S E R I E S

A life-changing encounter
with God's Word from the book of

DEUTERONOMY

NAVPRESS

Discipleship Inside Out™

NAVPRESS
Discipleship Inside Out™

NavPress is the publishing ministry of The Navigators, an international Christian organization and leader in personal spiritual development. NavPress is committed to helping people grow spiritually and enjoy lives of meaning and hope through personal and group resources that are biblically rooted, culturally relevant, and highly practical.

For a free catalog go to www.NavPress.com
or call 1.800.366.7788 in the United States or 1.800.839.4769 in Canada.

ISBN: 978-1-61521-642-0

Printed in the United States of America

1 2 3 4 5 6 7 8 / 16 15 14 13 12 11

CONTENTS

ACKNOWLEDGMENTS

The LifeChange series has been produced through the coordinated efforts of a team of Navigator Bible study developers and NavPress editorial staff, along with a nationwide network of field-testers.

SERIES EDITOR: KAREN LEE-THORP

HOW TO USE THIS STUDY

Objectives

Most guides in the LIFECHANGE series of Bible studies cover one book of the Bible. Although the LIFECHANGE guides vary with the books they explore, they share some common goals:

1. To provide you with a firm foundation of understanding and a thirst to return to the book
2. To teach you by example how to study a book of the Bible without structured guides
3. To give you all the historical background, word definitions, and explanatory notes you need so that your only other reference is the Bible
4. To help you grasp the message of the book as a whole
5. To teach you how to let God's Word transform you into Christ's image

Each lesson in this study is designed to take sixty to ninety minutes to complete on your own. The guide is based on the assumption that you are completing one lesson per week, but if time is limited, you can do half a lesson per week or whatever amount allows you to be thorough.

Flexibility

LIFECHANGE guides are flexible, allowing you to adjust the quantity and depth of your study to meet your individual needs. The guide offers many optional questions in addition to the regular numbered questions. The optional questions, which appear in the margins of the study pages, include the following:

Optional Application. Nearly all application questions are optional; we hope you will do as many as you can without overcommitting yourself.

For Thought and Discussion. Beginning Bible students should be able to handle these, but even advanced students need to think about them. These questions frequently deal with ethical issues and other biblical principles. They often offer cross-references to spark thought, but the references do not

7

give obvious answers. They are good for group discussions.

For Further Study. These include: (a) cross-references that shed light on a topic the book discusses, and (b) questions that delve deeper into the passage. You can omit them to shorten a lesson without missing a major point of the passage.

If you are meeting in a group, decide together which optional questions to prepare for each lesson and how much of the lesson you will cover at the next meeting. Normally, the group leader should make this decision, but you might let each member choose his or her own application questions.

As you grow in your walk with God, you will find the LifeChange guide growing with you—a helpful reference on a topic, a continuing challenge for application, a source of questions for many levels of growth.

Overview and details

The study begins with an overview of the book of Deuteronomy. The key to interpretation is context—what is the whole passage or book about?—and the key to context is purpose—what is the author's aim for the whole work? In lesson 1, you will lay the foundation for your study of Deuteronomy by asking yourself, *Why did the author (and God) write the book? What did they want to accomplish? What is the book about?*

Then, in lesson 2, you will begin analyzing successive passages of Deuteronomy in detail.

In lesson 13, you will review Deuteronomy, returning to the big picture to see whether your view of it has changed after closer study. Review will also strengthen your grasp of major issues and give you an idea of how you have grown from your study.

Each LifeChange guide is a little different, to suit the individual book. Deuteronomy is a long Old Testament book with fifteen chapters of laws for Israel (12:1–26:19). You may be excited to study what these laws can show you about God's character, Jesus' work, and our lives (see page 123 for an introduction to the laws). Or you may have only thirteen weeks to study Deuteronomy, so we've put seven optional lessons on the laws, organized by topic, in the back of this study guide. You might want to try one or two of them or come back to them later.

Kinds of questions

Bible study on your own—without a structured guide—follows a progression. First you *observe*: What does the passage say? Then you *interpret*: What does the passage mean? Lastly you *apply*: How does this truth affect my life?

Some of the "how" and "why" questions will take some creative thinking, even prayer, to answer. Some are opinion questions without clear-cut right answers; these will lend themselves to discussions and side studies.

Don't let your study become an exercise in knowledge alone. Treat the passages as God's Word, and stay in dialogue with Him as you study. Pray,

"Lord, what do You want me to see here?" "Father, why is this true?" "Lord, how does this apply to my life?"

It is important that you write down your answers. The act of writing clarifies your thinking and helps you remember.

Study aids

A list of reference materials, including a few notes of explanation to help you make good use of them, begins on page 216. This guide is designed to include enough background to let you interpret with just your Bible and the guide. Still, if you want more information on a subject or want to study a book on your own, try the references listed.

Scripture versions

Unless otherwise indicated, the Bible quotations in this guide are from the New International Version of the Bible. Another version cited is the New American Standard Bible (NASB).

Use any translation you like for study, preferably more than one. A paraphrase such as The Living Bible is not accurate enough for study, but it can be helpful for comparison or devotional reading.

Memorizing and meditating

A psalmist wrote, "I have hidden your word in my heart that I might not sin against you" (Psalm 119:11). If you write down a verse or passage that challenges or encourages you and reflect on it often for a week or more, you will find it beginning to affect your motives and actions. We forget quickly what we read once; we remember what we ponder.

When you find a significant verse or passage, you might copy it onto a card to keep with you. Set aside five minutes during each day just to think about what the passage might mean in your life. Recite it over to yourself, exploring its meaning. Then return to your passage as often as you can during your day for a brief review. You will soon find it coming to mind spontaneously.

For group study

A group of four to ten people allows the richest discussions, but you can adapt this guide for other-sized groups. It will suit a wide range of group types, such as home Bible studies, growth groups, youth groups, and businessmen's studies. Both new and mature Christians will benefit from the guide. You can omit any questions you find too easy and leave for later years any questions you find too hard.

The guide is intended to lead a group through one lesson per week. However, feel free to split lessons if you want to discuss them more thoroughly. Or omit some questions in a lesson if preparation or discussion time is limited. You can always return to this guide for personal study later. You will be able to discuss only a few questions at length, so choose some for discussion and others for background. Make time at each discussion for members to ask about anything they didn't understand.

Each lesson in the guide ends with a section called "For the group." This section gives advice on how to focus a discussion, how you might apply the lesson in your group, how you might shorten a lesson, and so on. The group leader should read each "For the group" at least a week ahead so that he or she can tell the group how to prepare for the next lesson.

Each member should prepare for a meeting by writing answers for all of the background and discussion questions to be covered. If the group decides not to take an hour per week for private preparation, then expect to take at least two meetings per lesson to work through the questions. Application will be very difficult, however, without private thought and prayer.

Two reasons for studying in a group are accountability and support. When each member commits in front of the rest to seek growth in an area of life, you can pray with one another, listen jointly for God's guidance, help one another to resist temptation, assure each other that the other's growth matters to you, use the group to practice spiritual principles, and so on. Pray about one another's commitments and needs at most meetings. Spend the first few minutes of each meeting sharing any results from applications prompted by previous lessons. Then discuss new applications toward the end of the meeting. Follow such sharing with prayer for these and other needs.

If you write down each other's applications and prayer requests, you are more likely to remember to pray for them during the week, ask about them at the next meeting, and notice answered prayers. You might want to get a notebook for prayer requests and discussion notes.

Notes taken during discussion will help you remember, follow up on ideas, stay on the subject, and clarify a total view of an issue. But don't let note-taking keep you from participating. Some groups choose one member at each meeting to take notes. Then someone copies the notes and distributes them at the next meeting. Rotating these tasks can help include people. Some groups have someone take notes on a large pad of paper or erasable marker board so that everyone can see what has been recorded.

Pages 219–220 list some good sources of counsel for leading group studies.

DEUTERONOMY TIMELINE[6]

2200 BC   2000   1800   1600   1400   1200   1000

OTHER NEAR EASTERN LAW CODES
(see page 65)

- Law code of Ur (Babylon)
- Law code of Hammurabi (Babylon)
- Hittite law codes
- Assyrian law code

ISRAEL

- Abraham
- Isaac
- Jacob/Israel
- Joseph
- Israel's family settles in Egypt
- Exodus (Sinai covenant)
- Moses' speeches in Moab (Deuteronomy)
- Fall of Jericho under Joshua
- (Judges)
- David

EGYPT

- 2134–1786 Middle Kingdom Egypt's secound most powerful period
- Israelites are slaves in Egypt
- 1570–1200 New Kingdom Egypt's greatest period

INTRODUCTION

Why Deuteronomy?

"Choose life, so that you and your children may live and that you may love the LORD your God, listen to his voice, and hold fast to him. For the LORD is your life."

Deuteronomy 30:19-20

Deuteronomy is one of the four Old Testament books most quoted in the New Testament, along with Genesis, Psalms, and Isaiah. Why is Deuteronomy so foundational to the New Testament?

Moses

First of all, Deuteronomy gives us the last words of Moses to the people he led for forty years. This man—born a Hebrew slave, adopted by an Egyptian princess, and raised as a prince—lost all hope of making his life a success when at age forty he killed an Egyptian in anger. He fled to the desert and kept sheep for forty years. Then God called Moses to lead His own sheep, the Israelites, out of bondage in Egypt. Moses obeyed, and for another forty years he guided this grumbling mob of fugitive slaves through the wilderness.

That long desert wandering was made necessary by the people's rebellion against God. But when we join the story in Deuteronomy, the whole original generation who left Egypt has died, and it is time for Israel to enter the land God promised to them. Because of his own disobedience, Moses himself is forbidden to lead Israel across the Jordan River into Canaan. Instead, Joshua, Moses' lieutenant, will lead the attack on the sophisticated, pagan cities of Canaan. So the people halt their march in Moab, just east of the river, to hear Moses' final words to them (see the map on page 36). His last three impassioned speeches are the book of Deuteronomy. These are the parting words of Israel's seasoned leader, the core of what he prayed Israel would remember, expressed with the emotion of one who knows what will happen if the people forget.

The treaty

Deuteronomy contains Moses' three speeches, but it is structured like an ancient Near Eastern treaty between an overlord and his vassal (a vassal is the chief of a subject clan or tribe; he makes treaties on behalf of his people). Deuteronomy formally states the *covenant* (treaty, pact, testament) between the Lord and Israel. In a way, Deuteronomy is the old covenant. If we want to understand "the new covenant" (Luke 22:20) that Jesus inaugurated and the New Testament describes, we must understand the old covenant that Deuteronomy summarizes.

God first declared His covenant with Israel at Mount Sinai, just after the people left Egypt (see Exodus 19:1–31:18). But after forty years in the desert, almost everyone who accepted the agreement at Sinai has died and a whole new generation has grown up. This generation knows of the oppression in Egypt, the miraculous deliverance, and the promises at Sinai only by report. Therefore, on the plains of Moab, Moses asks these people to reaffirm for themselves the covenant their parents made with the Lord.

None of the other nations in the Near East had treaties with their gods, so why did the Lord make one with Israel? Perhaps because it was the best way to express the relationship He wanted to have with His people.

The Law

The name *Deuteronomy* is Greek for "second law" (*deutero nomos*). The Greek translation of the Old Testament mistakenly renders Deuteronomy 17:18 as "this second law" instead of "a copy of this law." Deuteronomy is a "second law" only in that it repeats the Law for a new generation that was not present at Sinai.

In calling Deuteronomy "this [book of the] law" (30:10; 31:24,26), Moses does not intend it to be a "handbook"[1] for judges. Rather, "law" (Hebrew: *torah*) means "religious teaching given by a priest, a prophet or a wise man."[2] Deuteronomy expounds the faith that underlies Israel's desire to obey God. The book details God's faithfulness to Israel in the past (chapters 1–11) and in the future (chapters 12–34).[3] The covenant's basic assumption is that God's faithful care for Israel motivates Israel's faithful obedience to God. Therefore, Deuteronomy puts "laws" (in the narrow sense of rules of conduct) in the context of covenant love and faithfulness.

We can begin to see the relationship between laws and grace in the structure of the Near Eastern treaty that Deuteronomy follows:

1. A *historical prologue* recounts the Sovereign's unearned kindness (grace, mercy) toward the vassal. The prologue is meant to inspire gratitude (see Deuteronomy 1–3).
2. The *basic requirements* describe the relationship between Sovereign and vassal. (In Deuteronomy 4–11, we find words like "love" and "chose" frequently.)
3. The *specific rules of conduct* expected of the vassal (see Deuteronomy 12–26) are based on the Sovereign's past graciousness and the present relationship.

4. A clause requires the *recording* and sometimes the *renewal* of the covenant (see Deuteronomy 27,29).
5. *Blessings and curses* are promised for obedience and disobedience (see Deuteronomy 28).[4]

Old and new

Although Deuteronomy is the old covenant and we live under the new covenant, it still has much to say to us. As you look for ways to apply passages you are studying, consider the following facts:

1. The idea of a covenant or treaty with someone is unfamiliar to many modern people. Deuteronomy can show us what it means to have a *covenant relationship* with God.
2. *God's character* has not changed, so anything we observe about Him in Deuteronomy can help us know Him better. Deuteronomy shows us what God cares about, how He wants to treat people, how He wants people to treat people, and how He wants to be treated. The old covenant shows how high God's standards of justice and love are.
3. *Man's nature* has not changed, so Deuteronomy can show us what we are like.
4. The *ritual laws* of sacrifices and festivals are not renewed in the new covenant because Jesus fulfilled them in His self-sacrifice. We worship differently. However, the ritual laws do teach us what God is like, explain why Jesus' death was necessary, and show how it was effective. New Testament concepts like atonement, redemption, and holiness come from the old covenant.
5. The *civil laws* are not renewed in the new covenant, since they were designed for the civil state of Israel. However, they apply principles of justice that are still valid. They show us what God values, and they teach us by analogy what it means to love God and our neighbor. Few modern people know how much our own legal principles and procedures owe to Deuteronomy.
6. Some expectations of the old covenant are renewed in the new covenant. The *ethical laws* of Deuteronomy 6:5 and Leviticus 19:18, and the Ten Commandments (see Deuteronomy 5:6-21), which support them, are explicitly repeated and expanded upon in the New Testament. God still wants us to live by them, although we are no longer condemned if we fail.[5] (See the box "Law and Grace" on page 78.)

1. J. A. Thompson, Deuteronomy: *An Introduction and Commentary* (London: InterVarsity, 1974), 13.
2. Thompson, 12.
3. J. Sidlow Baxter, *Explore the Book* (Grand Rapids, MI: Zondervan, 1966), 212.
4. Thompson, 19.
5. Gordon Fee and Douglas Stuart, *How to Read the Bible for All Its Worth* (Grand Rapids, MI: Zondervan, 1982), 135–147. Christians understand the nature of the "new covenant" and the extent to which Old Testament laws should apply to us in widely different ways. You might ask your pastor how your church views these issues.

CHART OF DEUTERONOMY

Historical Prologue 1:1–3:29	First Speech	1 Promise and unbelief
		2 Conquest
		3 Land allotted; Moses' plea
Basic Stipulations 4:1–11:32	Second Speech	4 Listen and live; God's nature
		5 Ten Commandments: response to God's nature
		6 The Lord is One . . . Love the Lord
		7 Holy People
		8 Grace remembered
		9 Disobedience remembered
		10 Covenant remembered
		11 Covenant summary
Specific Cases 12:1–26:19		12 The place of worship
		13 Idolatry
		14 Clean food; tithes
		15 Release
		16 Feasts
		17 Leaders
		18 Tithes; prophecy
		19 Legal procedures
		20 Holy war
		21 Various laws
		22 Various laws
		23 Various laws
		24 Various laws
		25 Various laws
		26 Firstfruits
Document Clause		27 Covenant renewal ceremony
Blessings and Curses		28 Blessings and curses
Recapitulation 29:1–30:20	Third Speech	29 Recap: the things revealed
		30 Return and choose life
Transfer of Leadership 31:1–34:12		31 Transfer of authority
		32 Song of accusation
		33 Blessings
		34 Moses' death

The Near East in 1400 BC

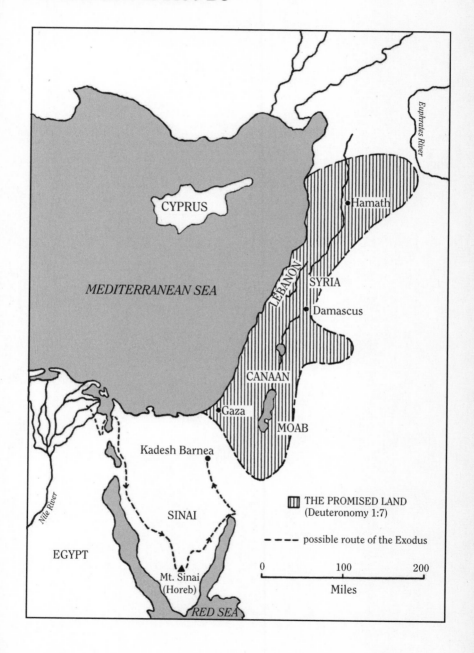

Euphrates River

CYPRUS

•Hamath

MEDITERRANEAN SEA

LEBANON

SYRIA

•Damascus

CANAAN

•Gaza

MOAB

Kadesh Barnea
•

▓ THE PROMISED LAND
(Deuteronomy 1:7)

- - - possible route of the Exodus

Nile River

SINAI

EGYPT

Mt. Sinai
(Horeb)

0   100   200

Miles

RED SEA

OVERVIEW

What Is Deuteronomy?

Bible teachers agree that it is important to do an overview of a book before studying it in detail. Because Deuteronomy is a long book, you might plan two weeks for the overview. This will give you plenty of time to absorb the "How to Use This Study" section on pages 7–10, the introduction on pages 13–17, and this first lesson. Many people find Deuteronomy intimidating at first glance, but it soon becomes manageable if taken gently at first. If you are studying with a group, see the "For the group" section on pages 25–27.

First impressions

If you have read the introduction on pages 13–17, you have some idea of what is in Deuteronomy. Still, there is no substitute for reading the book quickly yourself. If you spend ninety minutes doing this, you will have a much better sense of how particular passages fit into the whole work.

Use the chart on page 16 as a guide to the book's structure. The chart shows various ways of dividing Deuteronomy:

1. The far left column divides the book into the sections of a treaty to emphasize that this is the Sovereign Lord's covenant with Israel.
2. The center column shows where Moses begins and ends his three speeches. Notice that the first speech contains part of the basic requirements as well as the prologue.

3. The far right column suggests titles for each chapter of the book. Later in this study, you will make up your own titles.

For this overview, don't feel you must read every word of the book. In the upcoming questions, some important passages are suggested, but you need not limit yourself to these. The more effort you give to overview, the better prepared you will be for detailed study. Prayerfully consider the amount of the time you can devote to this.

The study guide allows space to answer questions, but if you want more room for further thoughts, optional questions, discussion notes, prayer requests, and plans for application, you can get a small notebook.

Most of the places named in Deuteronomy are on one of the maps on pages 17, 31, and 36.

1. Deuteronomy 1:1–3:29 is like the historical prologue in a treaty (see #1 on page 14); in it, Moses describes the Sovereign's unearned kindness toward His subjects.

   a. Read at least 1:1,19-46; 2:14-15,24-25,31-37. Of what events does Moses remind Israel?

   _____

   _____

   _____

   _____

   _____

   _____

   b. What can we learn about the Lord from these events?

   _____

   _____

   _____

   _____

   _____

2. In chapters 4–11, Moses states the basic things the Lord expects of Israel under the covenant.

   a. Read two or three of these passages: 4:1-8,32-35; 5:1-21; 6:4-9,20-25; 7:7-11; 9:4-6. What are some of the Lord's basic expectations? Notice the words that describe the covenant relationship between God and Israel (*love, choose* . . .) and those that describe God's expectations (*love, serve* . . .).

   _____

   _____

   _____

   _____

   _____

   _____

   b. What impressions of the Lord does this section give you?

   _____

   _____

   _____

   _____

   _____

3. The basic requirements of 4:1–11:32 are elaborated into specific laws in 12:1–26:19. Read a few of the laws, such as 15:12-18; 16:9-12,18-22; 19:15. (The chart on page 16, the subtitles in your Bible, and the optional lessons on pages 163–214 may help you find topics that interest you.)

   a. What kinds of matters do the laws cover?

   _____

   _____

For Further Study:
What do the
following verses
say about God's
nature: Deuteronomy
4:24,31,37; 5:8-10; 7:7-
9; 10:15-16; and 23:5?

_____

_____

_____

_____

_____

b. What do you observe about God (His justice,
   priorities, values, and so on)?

_____

_____

_____

_____

_____

_____

_____

4. Chapters 27–34 include a ceremony for
   renewing the covenant with each generation, a
   final exhortation to obey, and some things that
   happened when Moses transferred leadership to
   Joshua.
       Read at least 30:19-20; 31:24-32:7; 33:1-4.
   Notice on page 16 how these chapters fit into
   the treaty. What do you observe about God's
   character and the old covenant?

_____

_____

_____

_____

_____

_____

_____

_____

_____

5. From the introduction and your first reading, what would you say Deuteronomy is about? Summarize it in a sentence, or give the book your own title.

_____

_____

_____

Study Skill—Application

Second Timothy 3:16-17 tells us that *all* Scripture "is useful for teaching, rebuking, correcting and training in righteousness, so that the man of God may be thoroughly equipped for every good work." Romans 15:4 and 1 Corinthians 10:6,11 explain that Old Testament laws and history were recorded to teach, encourage, and warn us and to give us examples to follow. Therefore, the last step of Bible study is always to ask ourselves, *What difference should this passage make to my life? How should it make me want to think or act?* In your overview of Deuteronomy, you may have encountered:

1. An aspect of God's unchanging character. You can meditate (see page 9) on the verse or verses that show this aspect. Mull them over in your mind and ponder their significance. How should God's character affect the way you pray, treat your family, act at work, use your time or money, and so on? Write your conclusions and decisions in a notebook or the blank space at the end of this lesson. Tell someone what you decided.

2. An ethical principle repeated in the New Testament, such as 5:7-21. How can you apply this principle to your life this week?

3. A moral lesson from Israel's experience. How is it relevant to your life?

6. a. In your first reading of Deuteronomy, did you find anything you would like to commit to memory or apply? If so, what one truth would you like to concentrate on this week?

_____

_____

_____

_____

_____

_____

b. How can you apply this truth in your life? Try to think of at least one specific way.

_____

_____

_____

_____

_____

_____

7. As you skimmed Deuteronomy, you may have come across statements you'd like clarified or questions you'd like answered as you go deeper into this study. While your thoughts are still fresh, jot down your questions here to serve as personal objectives for your investigation of this book.

_____

_____

_____

_____

_____

_____

For the group

This "For the group" section and the ones in later lessons suggest ways of structuring your discussions. Feel free to select and adapt what suits your group.

Get acquainted. Because Deuteronomy is a long book, group members might appreciate two weeks to do the overview. If so, you can take a whole meeting to cover the following:

1. Ask the group to read "How to Use This Study" on pages 7–10 at home, but go over any important or difficult aspects as a group. Explain anything you think might be unfamiliar to the group. Let people ask questions about the study guide.

2. The beginning of a new study is a good time to lay a foundation for honest sharing of ideas, to get comfortable with each other, and to encourage a sense of common purpose. One way to establish common ground is to talk about what each member hopes to get out of your group—out of your study of Deuteronomy, and out of any prayer, singing, sharing, outreach, or anything else you might do together. Why are you studying the Bible, and Deuteronomy in particular? You can also discuss what you hope to give in your group. If you have someone write down each member's hopes and expectations, then you can look back at these goals later to see if they are being met.

It is important that everyone knows what the group is going to do and what he or she is supposed to do. Also, you will be better able to discuss personal application if you begin to establish trust.

Worship. Some groups like to begin their meetings with prayer and/or singing. Some share requests for prayer at the beginning, but leave the actual prayer until after the study. Others prefer just to chat and have refreshments for a while and then move to the study, leaving worship until the end.

Introduction. Here are some questions to ask the group, to remind everyone of the main points in the introduction (pages 13–16):

1. Where does the name *Deuteronomy* come from?

2. What does *Law (Torah)* mean?
3. What is a *covenant*?
4. In what ways is Deuteronomy like an ancient Near Eastern treaty between a sovereign and a vassal? Why is this important? Why did God make a treaty with Israel?
5. The book of Deuteronomy contains three speeches by Moses to Israel. Who was Moses? Where and when was he speaking? What was the purpose of this series of speeches?

Observations. Taking each section of the book in turn, ask someone to summarize what it is about. Then let group members state their observations and impressions (questions 1–4). When you have discussed each section, summarize what you have learned so far about (1) God's character and (2) the old covenant. These will be the focuses of the whole study.

Let each person share his or her summary or title of the book (question 5). If you begin with a clear idea of what you think the book is about, you have something to reconsider and revise as you study in detail.

Application. Ask specifically how Deuteronomy is relevant to your lives. If the group is unfamiliar with making applications, try this exercise together:

1. Pick a verse that seems relevant to you. For instance, look at Deuteronomy 8:3, which Jesus quotes in Luke 4:4.

2. State the truth that is relevant to you.

3. Describe in general how you fall short of what this verse teaches.

4. Name one specific way you can act on what this verse teaches. For Deuteronomy 8:3, you can make fifteen minutes in the Bible a priority each day before breakfast or lunch. Pray for the grace to do this so that you are not relying on your own resources. Plan to memorize 8:3 and meditate on it for further applications.

5. Decide how you can hold yourself account-able for keeping this commitment. For example, plan to come to your next meeting ready to tell on which days you had to miss breakfast to spend time in the Bible, on which days you had both devotions and breakfast, and on which days you chose food rather than Scripture. At that time, if necessary, the

group can help you assess whether your commitment was unreasonable or how you can change your schedule so that you will have time for both food and the Bible.

Questions. You may have questions about Deuteronomy that you can't answer yet. You can make a list of everyone's questions so that you can look for answers as you study. If this study guide and your reading of Deuteronomy can't answer a question, you might consult one of the references listed on pages 216–220 or ask your pastor for help.

Wrap-up. The group leader should have read through lesson 2 and its "For the group" section. At this point, he or she might give a one- or two-sentence summary of what members can expect in that lesson and in the coming meeting. This is a chance to whet everyone's appetite, assign any optional questions, omit any numbered questions, or forewarn members of any possible difficulties.

Worship. Many groups like to end with singing and/or prayer. This can include songs and prayers that respond to what you've learned in Deuteronomy, or prayers for specific needs of group members. Many people are shy about sharing personal needs or praying aloud in groups, especially before they know the group well. If this is true of your group, then a song and/or some silent prayer and a short closing prayer spoken by the leader might be an appropriate end. You might pray in pairs, if appropriate.

DEUTERONOMY 1:1–3:29

The Land

"See, I have given you this land. Go in and take possession of the land that the LORD swore he would give to your fathers—to Abraham, Isaac and Jacob—and to their descendants after them."
Deuteronomy 1:8

Memories are important to a relationship. Remembering how your dad forgave you even after you ruined something makes you eager to please him. Or remembering how he punished you makes you afraid. In Deuteronomy, Moses reminds the Israelites often of what they and God have done in the past. He wants them to remember their Father clearly—with a healthy respect, but also with gratitude and trust.

In 1:6–3:29, Moses recounts the history of Israel from the Sinai covenant to his current speech. The section parallels the historical prologue customary in a Near Eastern treaty (see "The Law" on page 14). As you study the section, think about why God might have wanted to remind the people of these events as a prelude to renewing His covenant with them. Try to put yourself in the place of the Israelites who had grown up as desert wanderers following the Lord and Moses.

Before you begin this lesson, you may want to look back at your overview of Deuteronomy. Then ask the Lord for wisdom, discernment, and concentration when you read through 1:1–3:29 (questions 1 and 2). Ask Him to reveal His character and His plan for Israel to you as you read.

For Further Study:
Could you retell the story of Israel's wandering, using questions 1 and 2 as a guide?

Desert east of Jordan . . . Dizahab (1:1). Moses preached the sermons of Deuteronomy somewhere near Mt. Nebo (see the map on page 31).

Expound this law (1:5). At Sinai, God has already given His instruction about who He is and how Israel should live. The covenant at Moab renews for a new generation the covenant made at Sinai. Deuteronomy 1:1-5 explains the book's setting.

Horeb (1:2,6). See the map on page 17. The name comes from the Hebrew word for "desolation." Deuteronomy uses this name for Mt. Sinai.

Study Skill—Reading
Questions 1 and 2 each ask you to read the whole passage. Rereading is the best way to observe many details and grasp the overall message of the passage, but if your time is limited, you can try to do questions 1 and 2 with one reading.

---

1. Read 1:1–3:29 through for a general impression of it. As you read, keep a list of the words and phrases that appear over and over. (In his speeches, Moses repeats the key words he wants the people to remember about their history.)

mountain, your fathers

_____

_____

_____

_____

_____

_____

_____

The Promised Land

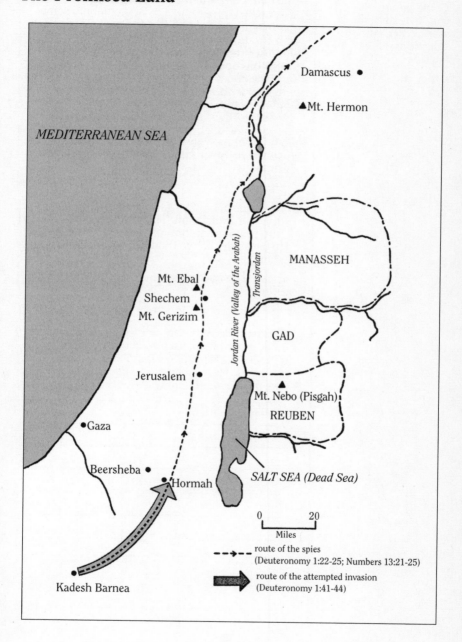

MEDITERRANEAN SEA

Damascus ●

▲ Mt. Hermon

MANASSEH

Jordan River (Valley of the Arabah)

Transjordan

Mt. Ebal ▲
Shechem ●
Mt. Gerizim ▲

GAD

Jerusalem ●

Mt. Nebo (Pisgah) ▲

REUBEN

● Gaza

Beersheba ●

Hormah

SALT SEA (Dead Sea)

0   20
Miles

- - - → route of the spies
(Deuteronomy 1:22-25; Numbers 13:21-25)

➡ route of the attempted invasion
(Deuteronomy 1:41-44)

Kadesh Barnea

2. Now read 1:1–3:29 again, preferably in a different translation. This time break the section into passages according to where Moses seems to pause or change thought. Give each passage a short title.

   1:1-5 _Introduction_ _____

   _____

   _____

   _____

   _____

   _____

   _____

   _____

   _____

   _____

   _____

   _____

   _____

Lord (1:6). The personal name of the God of Israel. Written Hebrew lacked vowels in Moses' day, so the name is written YHWH. It means "I AM WHO I AM" (Exodus 3:14). That is, YHWH is the One who is actively present with His people. He revealed Himself by this name (I AM Myself; I AM with you—see Exodus 3:12; 34:6-7) in the deliverance from Egypt.

If the Divine Name ever had a pronunciation, it has been forgotten. The Jews came to regard it as too holy to be spoken; in reading the Scriptures, they began to substitute the word *Lord* (Hebrew: *Adonai*) for the name. Most English translations follow this custom, writing "the LORD" instead of transliterating the name. Some translations write "Jehovah," which adds the vowels of *Adonai* to the consonants of YHWH (JHVH). Others write "Yahweh" or "Jahveh," guessing at the original pronunciation. This study guide speaks of "the Lord." However, remember that Moses was freely using God's personal name.

Sovereign Lord (3:24). "Lord GOD" in NASB. Here "LORD" is YHWH, and "Sovereign" renders the Hebrew *Adonai*, which means "my lord, sovereign, master."

3. a. What does Moses say about God in each of the following verses?

1:10 _____

_____

1:11 _____

_____

33

Optional Application: How can the observations you recorded in question 3 affect the way you treat or respond to God? Write some specific ways in question 7, in the margin here, or on the blank space at the end of this chapter.

1:17 _____

_____

1:19 _____

_____

1:25 _____

_____

_____

1:30 _____

_____

1:31 _____

_____

2:7 _____

_____

3:24 _____

_____

_____

_____

_____

_____

_____

_____

b. What impression of God do you get from these verses?

_____

_____

_____

_____

_____

_____

_____

_____

_____

Take possession (1:6-8)

Study Skill—Types

A *type* is an Old Testament person, object, or event that prefigures its *antitype* in the Messianic Age (New Testament times and after). God gave types to prepare Israel to understand Christ and to be moral and doctrinal examples for us (see 1 Corinthians 10:6,11; Hebrews 10:1). In some cases the New Testament explicitly states that something in the Old Testament is a type (see Hebrews 7:3; 9:8-9; 11:19; 1 Peter 3:21). At other times it does not. Some interpreters fall into error by abusing typology, but we can avoid foolish mistakes if we keep some principles in mind:

1. "No doctrine or theory should ever be built upon a type or types independently of direct teaching elsewhere in Scripture." Types are meant to illustrate, amplify, and illuminate doctrines taught explicitly elsewhere.

2. "The parallelism between type and antitype should not be pressed to fanciful extremes."[1]

The New Testament explicitly says that the Promised Land is a type of a "country" that Christians "inherit." Just as the Promised Land is called Israel's "inheritance" in the Old Testament (see Deuteronomy 3:28; 4:21,38), so Christians have an "inheritance" (Ephesians 1:13-14,18). Therefore, if we take care not to press this parallelism too far, we can learn something about our own inheritance and mission from Deuteronomy. Ask God to give you discernment to see what applies to you and what does not.

Regions of Canaan

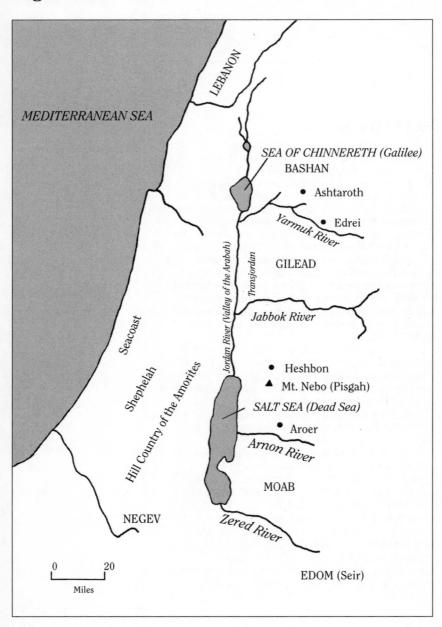

The hill country of the Amorites . . . (1:7). See
the maps on pages 31 and 36. Deuteronomy
1:7 gives the dimensions of the Promised Land
according to its main geographical divisions.
The area Moses names is far "larger than Israel
ever possessed in fact, even during the reigns of
David and Solomon."[2]

    The hill country . . . the mountains.
("The mount of the Amorites" and "the hills"
in KJV.) The central mountainous area of
Palestine that runs north-south.

    The Arabah. ("The plain" in KJV.) The
rift valley from the Sea of Chinnereth (Galilee)
to the Gulf of Aqaba. The Jordan River flows
through the Arabah.

    The western foothills. ("Lowland" in
NASB and RSV; "vale" or low country" in KJV.)
Literally "The Shephelah."[3] This is a range
of low hills west of the hill country of the
Amorites.

    The Negev. ("The south" in KJV.) The
semi-desert and desert region south of the hill
country and the Shephelah.

    All of the above area was ***the land of the
Canaanites*** in Moses' day. ***Lebanon*** is north of
the land of the Canaanites, and ***the Euphrates***
River is northeast of Lebanon.

---

4. God promised to give His people the land of
   Canaan (see Deuteronomy 1:8). What "land" has
   He promised that Christians will inherit? (Look
   at a few of the following: Matthew 5:3,5; Luke
   18:18; Philippians 3:20-21; 1 Thessalonians 4:15-
   17; Hebrews 11:13-16; Revelation 21:1-4.)

   _____

   _____

   _____

   _____

   _____

   _____

   _____

5. At the time of Moses' speech in Moab, Israel had
   already received a down payment of the whole
   Promised Land (see Deuteronomy 2:24–3:20).
   Likewise, the church has received a down
   payment and guarantee of its inheritance (see
   Luke 17:20-21; Ephesians 1:13-14). In what sense
   do we already possess our inheritance?

   _____

   _____

   _____

   _____

   _____

6. However, like Israel, we also await the full
   enjoyment of our inheritance. In part, we wait
   in faith for God to act. In this sense we are like
   Abraham. Yet, in another sense God invites us to
   "take possession" of the Promised Land.
      How can we participate in the church's
   mission to take possession of the earth as God's
   kingdom? Choose one or more of the following
   verses:

   Philippians 2:12-13 _____

   _____

   _____

   _____

   _____

   _____

   Matthew 28:18-20; 2 Timothy 2:1-7; 4:1-2 _____

   _____

   _____

   _____

   _____

   _____

Ephesians 6:10-20 _____

_____

_____

_____

_____

Optional Application: Imagine the prologue to your own covenant (agreement about relationship) with the Lord. What history might He include to remind you of how He has acted in your life? Name at least three key events in your relationship so far. (Use your own notebook or blank space at the end of this book.)

Study Skill—Application

An application can grow from examining a passage with two questions: "Who is God?" and "What does He ask of Me?" The trick is to consider these questions long and prayerfully enough so that you think of something *specific* that you can actually do or impress on your heart. For example, if you meditated on 1:30-31 and 2:7 for a while, you might have made the following decision:

"Because the Lord is our God who fights for us, I will ask Him to victoriously bring Donna and Steve into His kingdom. I will participate in this battle by praying daily for them and for opportunities to testify that my God is the one who has carried me 'as a father carries his son' (1:31) and who has been with me so that I have lacked nothing (2:7). To remember these things, I will meditate on 1:30-31 and 2:7 this week."

7. a. Reread what you learned about God in question 3 and about our mission in questions 4–6. Is there one truth from these that you would like to put into practice this week? If so, what insight would you like to apply?

_____

_____

_____

_____

_____

_____

b. What specific steps can you take to act on this truth?

_____

_____

_____

_____

8. List any questions you have about anything covered in this lesson.

_____

_____

_____

_____

For the group

Worship.

Warm-up. This lesson and the next cover the historical prologue to Deuteronomy, in which Moses reminds the Israelites of their past relationship with the Lord. This history shows how the Lord has been faithful to Israel and why Israel should be loyal to Him.

To help group members see the point of this prologue and get to know each other, you could take five or ten minutes to let everyone who wants to do so share one event in his or her life when the Lord has shown His covenant faithfulness. It could be a time when He took care of them, delivered them from a predicament, stuck with them despite sin, or disciplined them. (See the "Optional Application" on page 39.) Or you could ask, "What one memory of your earthly father could you share that would illustrate his character for the rest of us?"

Reading. It's always a good idea to read the passage before you discuss it. Someone might be present who hasn't prepared the lesson, and many people may have forgotten it. However, in many lessons of this study, you will be covering several chapters. When that happens, you may decide to allow ten minutes for everyone to read the passage silently or to read parts of it aloud. You can divide the passage among several readers, each reading several paragraphs or half a chapter.

Overview. Allow about ten minutes to summarize the main points of Moses' prologue. First, quickly list the speech's key words (question 1), and then recount the main events Moses describes (question 2). Try to make the story real and vivid.

Details. Use the observe-interpret-apply progression to organize your discussion. For instance, first observe what the verses in question 3 say about God, then discuss what some of them mean, and finally discuss how they are relevant to your lives. Then observe what the verses in question 4 say about our inheritance, interpret what they mean, and apply them in specific ways to yourselves.

Always ask whether the information in a study skill is unfamiliar to anyone in the group and whether anyone has questions about the skill. Draw attention to how the lesson applies the skill. The goal is for the group to become able to use these skills in study without a study guide.

Some people may have difficulty grasping the concept that our inheritance is both something we already have and something we do not yet have in its fullness. Discuss how our inheritance (the kingdom of God, salvation, eternal life, the promised country) is both present and yet to come. Try not to sidetrack the whole meeting to this topic, but make sure it is clear. It is a central teaching of the New Testament.

Application. Before you address application, look at the section titled "Old and new" on page 15 and the "Study Skill—Application" on page 39. If the discussion seems to be taking a tangent that contradicts the study guide's suggestions, you might stop and discuss whether you accept its suggestions and how they apply to the issue at hand.

In later lessons, "For Thought and Discussion" and "Optional Application" questions in the margins

41

give some suggestions about how to apply Israel's lessons to yourselves. If everyone has prepared the written questions on this passage, you should be able to spend half of your discussion time on application. Look for an application from each episode in turn, but don't force an application from an episode that has none.

Encourage group members to find at least one application that seems especially relevant to themselves. Give everyone a chance (but don't pressure anyone) to share: "The main implication I think this lesson has for my life is . . . In response I am going to . . . this week." Encourage group members to think about what they can do to let the implications of 1:1–3:29 affect their lives or whether they need to make a prayer priority of trusting God to do something. You might spend a few minutes in silent prayer and reflection.

If group members are finding the writing space in the study guide too limited, suggest that they write in the margins, on blank space at the end of the guide, or in a separate notebook. Many people like to keep a prayer and application notebook even while using a study guide.

Prayer. Your closing prayer could begin with thanks to God for His faithfulness in your histories and for the example of Israel's experience to guide you. Then ask Him to enable you to learn from that history and to respond to Him as Israel should have responded. Ask for grace to do anything you believe you need to do.

1. J. Sidlow Baxter, *Explore the Book* (Grand Rapids, MI: Zondervan, 1966), 53–56.
2. Peter C. Craigie, *The Book of Deuteronomy* (Grand Rapids, MI: Eerdmans, 1976), 95.
3. Craigie, 95; Yohanan Aharoni, *The Land of the Bible: A Historical Geography*, trans. A. F. Rainey (Philadelphia: Westminster, 1962), 38.

DEUTERONOMY 1:9–3:29

Reminders

*"See, the L*ORD *your God has given you the land. Go up and take possession of it as the L*ORD, *the God of your fathers, told you. Do not be afraid; do not be discouraged."*

Deuteronomy 1:21

What a rich land God had promised Israel! What a glorious mission the nation had: "Go up and take possession of it"! Wouldn't you have been eager to start, afraid of nothing with God at your side?

Israel wasn't. The people were anxious when they should have been bold, and rash when they should have been patient. Moses, who would not be there to lead in the coming battles, wanted to press home the lessons those early experiences should have taught. His words are sound reminders for us to our service to God.

Look back at questions 1 and 2 on pages 30 and 32. If necessary, reread 1:1–3:29.

Sin and consequences (1:19–2:23)

1. Immediately after making the Sinai covenant, God commanded Israel to march straight to the Promised Land (see 1:6-8). How did the people respond at first?

   1:19 _____

   _____

   2:22 _____

   _____

**Optional
Application:** a. Have
you ever been afraid
of obeying direction
from the Lord despite
promises from Him? If
so, what did you fear?
   b. What
encouragement
and warning does
1:19–3:11 offer people
in this situation?

Through all that vast and dreadful desert (1:19).
   It was over a hundred miles long, through an
   almost waterless plateau.[1]

2. The spies confirmed that the land of Canaan
   was good (see 1:25). Nevertheless, the people did
   not want to enter it (see 1:26). How did they sin
   in their attitude toward God (see 1:27-28)?

   _____

   _____

   _____

   _____

   _____

3. Why should they have trusted the Lord (see
   1:30-31,33)?

   _____

   _____

   _____

   _____

   _____

4. What happened because of the people's sin (see
   1:34-40; 2:14-15)?

   _____

   _____

   _____

   _____

   _____

_____

_____

5. Observe how the people responded to their punishment (see 1:41). Why did they fail when they tried to obey the Lord's original command (see 1:42-46)?

_____

_____

_____

_____

_____

6. Reread your answers to questions 1–5 and the "Optional Application" on page 44. What lessons does 1:19-46, 2:14-15 have for our lives?

_____

_____

_____

_____

_____

_____

_____

_____

_____

Victory (2:24–3:11)

When the spies brought back news about the Amorites in Canaan, the Israelites were afraid (see

Study Skill—
Interpreting Old Testament Narratives

A narrative is a story. When we read a biblical narrative, we are reading a true story about God as He revealed Himself to a line of people over centuries. Here are some principles for interpreting any biblical narrative, particularly Old Testament ones as in Deuteronomy:

1. Not every episode in Israel's history is meant to teach an individual moral lesson. Sometimes a story is significant only as part of the whole history of God's dealings with Israel. However, we can usually learn something about God from most episodes.

2. Narratives record what happened, not necessarily what ought to happen every time. So again, a particular episode may have its own moral. (For instance, the way God divided the land in Deuteronomy 3:12-20 has a point only in the context of the whole story. It was a one-time event.)

3. Not every detail of a narrative has deep significance. The point may be in the overall message. However, the point of an episode may not be obvious unless we carefully observe many details.

4. A narrative may teach "implicitly" (by clearly implying something without actually stating it). However, we should be wary of teachers who see "hidden" meanings that other Christians do not see. (There probably aren't mystical meanings to the divisions in 3:12-20, and the kings in 2:26 and 3:1 probably don't symbolize future figures.)

5. "*All* narratives are selective and incomplete. Not all the relevant details are always given (see John 21:25). What does appear in the narrative is everything that the inspired author thought important for us to know." We must be content with our curiosity unsatisfied.

6. "Narratives are not written to answer all our theological questions. They have particular, specific, limited purposes and deal with certain issues, leaving others to be dealt with elsewhere, in other ways."

7. God is the main character (the hero) of all biblical narratives. The human beings are always secondary characters in a story about what God did.[2]

1:28). The Amorites were a tall, strong people living in cities with high, thick walls. They were undoubtedly better armed than the Israelites, and their defensive position was excellent. However, forty years after the Israelites were miserably defeated by these warriors (see 1:42-46), Israel easily conquered Heshbon (see 2:24-37) and Bashan (see 3:1-11). The maps on pages 31 and 36 show the territory that Israel captured east of the Jordan River and how it was divided among the tribes (see 3:8-17). Notice the conditions Moses placed on their use of this land (see 3:18-20).

For Thought and Discussion: What is wrong with assuming that just because you are a Christian you will win at whatever you want to win at? Support your answer from Scripture if possible.

7. How was it possible for the Israelites to defeat foes far stronger than they (see 2:25,33)?

_____

_____

_____

_____

_____

8. The Lord did not approve every battle Israel fought or wanted to fight (see 1:41-46; 2:2-9). What do you think His permission (and enablement) to conquer some people and not others taught Israel about Him?

_____

_____

_____

_____

_____

_____

9. How are the lessons of Deuteronomy 2:24–3:11 relevant to our lives as Christians engaged in

For Further Study:
Study Hebrews 3:7–
4:11. What is the rest
of God, and how can
you enter into it?

spiritual warfare (see Ephesians 6:12)?

_____

_____

_____

_____

_____

_____

Rest (3:20). Peace from external threat, internal
conflict, famine, or plague.[3] This was temporarily and partially fulfilled four hundred years
later in the time of Solomon (see Joshua 1:13;
2 Samuel 7:1,11; 1 Kings 5:4). However, rest
has deeper meanings from Genesis 2:2-3 and
Exodus 20:8-11. The writer to the Hebrews sees
the rest Moses promised Israel as a type of the
Sabbath-rest of God available to God's people
(see Hebrews 3:7–4:11).

Leadership (1:9-18; 3:23-29)

If your time is limited, you can omit part or all of
this section.

Because of you the LORD was angry with me
(1:37; 3:26). Moses had been a faithful and righteous leader for forty years, yet God answered
no to his fervent prayer. Moses had to pay the
price for a sin he committed at Meribah less
than a year before the speeches of Deuteronomy
(see Numbers 20:1-13). In exasperation at
Israel's whining, Moses had disobeyed the
Lord's precise command by striking the rock at
Meribah instead of speaking to it. This angry
act offended God's holiness and even suggested
that Moses was not fully relying on God to sup-
ply Israel's needs.[4]

10. At Meribah, Moses had acted as though he, not the Lord, was responsible for Israel. But the Lord had never intended Moses to be Israel's sole leader. He had given subordinates to Moses at Horeb (see Exodus 18:13-26; Deuteronomy 1:9-18).

For Further Study: Read Numbers 20:1-13 and Deuteronomy 3:23-28. What can we learn from these incidents about God's character, human leadership, and prayer?

a. Why is it important for a leader to share responsibility (see Deuteronomy 1:9,12)?

_____

_____

_____

_____

_____

_____

b. What were Moses' assistants appointed to do (see 1:15-16)?

_____

_____

_____

_____

c. What traits did Moses seek in them (see 1:13,15)?

_____

_____

_____

_____

d. Who chose them (see 1:13)?

_____

_____

_____

_____

e. According to what standard were they supposed to judge, and why (see 1:16-17)?

_____

_____

_____

_____

_____

11. a. To what extent is 1:13-18 a model for choosing Christian leaders?

_____

_____

_____

_____

_____

_____

b. To what extent is it not a model because circumstances are different?

_____

_____

_____

_____

_____

_____

_____

_____

12. What do you think is the purpose of the historical prologue? That is, why do you think God reminded His people of the history in 1:6–3:29 before renewing His covenant with them?

_____

_____

_____

_____

_____

The Torah today

For Thought and Discussion: How should we go about deciding how lessons from Old Testament stories apply to our lives? (Consider, for instance, selecting leaders or conquering land.)

(continued from page 51)

Thus, we should not try to copy everything even a great man such as Moses or David does in a narrative, nor do everything God tells someone to do. We should let the rest of Scripture, especially the New Testament, guide us in drawing lessons.

3. We are not always told at the end of a narrative whether what happened was good or bad. We are expected to be able to judge that on the basis of what God has taught us directly elsewhere in the Scriptures.

4. In every case, God is speaking to or dealing with a particular person. In 1:8 he tells Israel to "take possession"; in 2:9 He says the opposite. Which command, if either, applies to us today? If the former, do Israel's particular tactics of frontal military assault apply to us also?

Instead of looking for tactics to copy, we should focus on God's character, His aims, and the variety of His methods. When we feel led to apply a specific command such as "Take possession" or "You shall wander in the desert forty years," we should seek discernment from the Holy Spirit and counsel from other Christians.

5. If God's Word illustrates a *principle* the New Testament would uphold, we can apply the principle to *genuinely comparable* situations in our own lives. Our task is to discern the principle accurately and see that our situations are truly comparable.

Thus, we must earnestly seek discernment and wisdom from the Holy Spirit and use the New Testament to guide us.[6]

13. a. Think about God's character, how He deals with Israel, and what He expects from His people. What one insight from your study of 1:1–3:29 would you like to apply to some situation you are facing?

_____

_____

_____

_____

_____

_____

_____

b. How can you apply this insight to your life? Write down how it is relevant and anything you plan to do about it (prayer, meditation on some passage, a specific action or decision).

_____

_____

_____

_____

_____

14. List any questions you have about 1:1–3:29.

_____

_____

_____

_____

Optional Application: This study may have impressed you more with truths about God and His people than with action you need to take immediately. If so, write down in question 13 a verse or verses from 1:1–3:29 that you want to let sink into your mind and heart. Set aside time each day for the next week to meditate on these verses, even as you go on to lesson 4 of this study. Reflect on the implications of these verses for your attitudes in your life. (See the paragraph on page 9 on memorizing and meditating.)
 You might choose one of the following passages: 1:16-17; 1:21; 1:29-31.

For the group

Worship.

Warm-up. Take a few minutes to share how your efforts to apply something in lesson 2 have gone. Does anyone have any questions or frustrations? On page 75 are some common obstacles to application that people face, along with some suggested solutions. You can help each other with application by praying for each other, offering gentle counsel, and encouraging each other. Strive not to make another feel guilty about failure, but do help one another face failure and learn from it. Don't expect to see dramatic changes in your lives overnight (see 7:22-23), but trust the Lord.

Read aloud. Have different people read 1:9-18; 1:19–2:23; 2:24–3:11; 3:23-29.

Summarize. Ask someone to remind the group what 1:1–3:29 is about. Reading and summarizing are excellent ways to refresh everyone's memory and bring previously absent members up to date.

Details. Use the observe-interpret-apply progression to study each section of the prologue. First, observe important details.[7] Questions 1–5 do this for 1:19-20. Ask extra observation questions to point out other details, if necessary.

Next, draw out the lessons you think Moses wanted Israel to learn from the history he chose to recall. For instance, what should Israel have learned from the episode of the spies (see 1:19-46)? From their desert wandering (see 2:1-23)? From their victories (see 2:24–3:11)? From the appointment of leaders (see 1:9-18)? From God's discipline to Moses (see 3:23-29)? Try to find and write down one key lesson from each scene you deal with. Look for a consistent thread or theme throughout the prologue. Finally, discuss how the lessons of each section apply to you personally.

You may decide not to try to cover all of these episodes but to focus on one, two, or three of them.

Wrap-up. Your closing prayer could begin with thanks to God for the example of Israel's experience to guide you. Then ask Him to enable you to learn from history and to respond to Him as Israel should have responded. Ask for grace to do anything you believe you need to do.

1. Peter C. Craigie, *The Book of Deuteronomy* (Grand Rapids, MI: Eerdmans, 1976),100.
2. Gordon Fee and Douglas Stuart, *How to Read the Bible for All Its Worth* (Grand Rapids, MI: Zondervan, 1982), 74–75, 78.
3. Kenneth Barker, ed., *The NIV Study Bible* (Grand Rapids, MI: Zondervan, 1985), 249.
4. Barker, 220, 246.
5. Fee and Stuart, 24.
6. Fee and Stuart, 78.
7. In deciding what is important, you are doing interpretation, of course.

DEUTERONOMY 4:1-43

Reasons to Obey

"What other nation is so great as to have their gods near them the way the LORD our God is near us whenever we pray to him? And what other nation is so great as to have such righteous decrees and laws as this body of laws I am setting before you today?"
Deuteronomy 4:7-8

As children, we learned that being good meant obeying the rules. God had lots of rules for His Israelite children, but it mattered to Him that they obey for the right reasons. Otherwise, they would always be looking for ways to get around the rules and, worst of all, resenting their Father for making the rules. Neither disobedience nor obedience for the wrong reasons would ever lead to the relationship God wanted.

In chapters 1–3, Moses laid out the history of the relationship between God and Israel since their formal covenant. In chapter 4, he ends his first speech with an exhortation to remember all the reasons for obeying God. Chapters 4–11 correspond to the section of a treaty that covers the overlord's basic expectations of the vassal.

1. a. Read 4:1-43 prayerfully. Overall, what is this passage about? (Give a title or short summary.)

   _____

   _____

For Thought and Discussion: a. Why is 4:2 often difficult to obey? (Perhaps you can think of a time when you have disobeyed this instruction.)

b. Consider memorizing Deuteronomy 4:2 and keeping it in mind when you study Scripture. Compare this verse to Revelation 22:18-19.

For Thought and Discussion: How does 4:3-4 illustrate the Deuteronomic principle?

b. (*Optional*) Make a rough outline of 4:1-43 by dividing it into paragraphs and giving each a title.

_____

_____

_____

_____

_____

_____

_____

The Deuteronomic principle

(4:1-4,25-28,40)

2. Verses 4:1,40 state what has been called the Deuteronomic principle[1] because Moses repeats it so many times in this book. The principle is that . . .

Israel should _____

_____

so that _____

_____

3. Deuteronomy 4:25-28 states the principle negatively. It says . . .

If_____

_____

_____

then_____

_____

_____

56

4. The God of Justice ordains consequences that fit their causes (see Deuteronomy 19:21; Galatians 6:7). What is ironic or suitable about the consequence Deuteronomy 4:28 promises for the sin of 4:25?

_____

_____

_____

_____

Optional Application: How does Deuteronomy 4:16-20,25,28 apply to our lives? What things do we idolize, and what results from that choice?

Optional Application: How does 4:6-8 apply to Christians?

A wise nation (4:6-8)

5. Moses gives a second reason for obedience in 4:6: "This will show your wisdom and understanding to the nations." Why will the nations consider Israel wise and understanding?

4:7 _____

_____

_____

4:8 _____

_____

_____

6. Many Christians regard the Old Testament Law as more a burden than a blessing. Why was the Law a gracious gift? (*Optional*: See Psalm 1:1-6; 19:7-11; 119:1-176.)

_____

_____

_____

_____

_____

For Further Study:
Exodus 19:1–20:26
tells more about
the event Moses
mentions in
Deuteronomy 4:10.

God's mighty acts (4:9-10,15,20,32-38)

7. a. In 4:9, Moses exhorts the people to not forget
   what they have seen and to teach these
   memories to their children. What crucial
   experience are they supposed to remember
   (see 4:10)?

   _____

   _____

   b. What was most important about that event
      (see 4:9-18)?

   _____

   _____

   _____

   _____

   _____

8. What events to be remembered does 4:32-38
   add?

   _____

   _____

   _____

   _____

   _____

   _____

Relationship

9. Why did God perform these unprecedented
   deeds for Israel?

   4:10 _____

   4:20 _____

   _____

58

4:35,39 _____

_____

_____

_____

Optional Application: Choose one of Israel's reasons to obey God that you think applies to you. Meditate on it daily this week, and look for ways to worship and obey God.

Jealous (4:24). Because He is utterly holy, God is zealous for active righteousness and cannot tolerate allegiance to a less-than-holy god. Because He loves Israel, He demands that Israel respond with faithful covenant love (see 6:5).[2]

10. Tell in your own words what Moses says about God in 4:24,31?

_____

_____

_____

_____

_____

_____

11. Now summarize God's character and attributes as questions 7–10 have revealed them.

_____

_____

_____

_____

_____

_____

_____

_____

12. In summary, list at least three reasons from 4:1-40 why Israel should obey God.

a. _____

_____

b. _____

_____

c. _____

_____

The Torah today

The Deuteronomic principle states the essence of the Law—as predictable, certain, and just as the law of gravity. Galatians 6:7 states that it still operates in our lives, whether we are Christians or not. It was meant to assure us blessing when we obey God, but when we sin we force the Deuteronomic principle to act against us (see Romans 7:9-13).

> **Study Skill—Cross-References**
> It is important to study the Old Testament in light of the New. Cross-references—other passages of Scripture—will help you do this.

13. a. What effect does the Deuteronomic principle have on a sinful person (see Romans 6:23; Galatians 6:8)?

_____

_____

_____

_____

b. How can a person escape the ultimate consequences of sin (see Romans 8:1-4;

Hebrews 9:19-22,28; 1 John 1:9; Isaiah 53:4-6)?

_____

_____

_____

_____

c. Does this mean that a Christian no longer bears any consequences for his sins? Why or why not (see Romans 8:13; 1 Corinthians 6:16-18; Galatians 5:15; 6:7-9)?

_____

_____

_____

_____

_____

_____

14. Review the reasons for obedience you wrote in question 12. Which of them do you think apply to Christians, and why? (For instance, should fear of punishment still motivate us in light of the way of escape you explained in the second part of question 13?)

_____

_____

_____

_____

_____

_____

_____

For Further Study:
Study the following cross-references for reasons why Christians should obey God: John 14:23; 15:5-6; 2 Corinthians 5:14-15; Ephesians 5:1-2; Hebrews 10:26-31,35-36; 1 Peter 2:12; 1 John 4:7-12.

Study Skill—Application

You can approach application in different ways at different times. At one time, you can list as many personal implications of some passage as you can. You can return to this list frequently over the following week to see if you need to confess, pray, or act regarding any of them. At another time, you can deeply explore just one implication of a passage, planning a specific response and praying for grace.

Some people like to use these five questions when looking for an application:

Is there a *sin* for me to avoid?

Is there a *promise* for me to trust?

Is there an *example* for me to follow?

Is there a *command* for me to obey?

How can this passage increase my *knowledge* of the Lord (not just knowledge about Him)?

You can recall these five questions by remembering the acronym SPECK—Sin, Promise, Example, Command, Knowledge.

15. a. Review this lesson and read the "Optional Application" questions in it. What one truth from Deuteronomy 4:1-43 would you like to concentrate on in your own life?

_____

_____

_____

_____

_____

_____

_____

b. How should this truth affect your attitudes, actions, and current decisions? (Or how does your life fall short of this truth?)

_____

_____

62

_____

_____

_____

c. What specific action (including prayer and meditation) can you take to put this truth into practice?

_____

_____

_____

_____

16. List any questions you have about 4:1-43.

_____

_____

_____

_____

_____

For Thought and Discussion: Paul called the Christian way of life "the obedience that comes from faith" (Romans 1:5). How is this obedience like what you have seen so far of the obedience Moses preached?

Cities (4:41-43). Cities of refuge were going to be necessary during Israel's transition from nomadic (wandering) to settled life. Nomadic tribes considered killing to be an offense against the family of the one killed. The dead man's nearest relative was expected to avenge the death by killing the killer (and often his family also). This relative was called "the avenger of blood" (19:6)

God's Law gave procedures for distinguishing between intentional and accidental manslaughter (see 19:1-13). To prevent the avenger from spilling innocent blood, Moses designated cities where a person could be safe until his trial.

a. Sometimes talking, confessing, or praying with another Christian helps to impress an insight from Scripture onto our hearts. Is there anyone with whom you could share your insights from Deuteronomy 4:1-43?

b. Meditation is a way of setting the mind "on what the Spirit desires" (Romans 8:5). Consider meditating on Deuteronomy 4:2; 4:7-8; 4:9; 4:24; 4:29; 4:31; 4:32-35; or 4:39-40.

For the group

Warm-up. Moses said that the Lord spoke to Israel and worked miracles of deliverance "so that you might know that the LORD is God; besides him there is no other" (Deuteronomy 4:35). You might begin your meeting by letting everyone who wants to briefly share one thing the Lord has done to show him or her that "the LORD is God in heaven above and on the earth below. There is no other." (4:39).

Observation. You can structure this meeting by asking group members to list all the reasons for obedience that they found in chapter 4. Then go back and discuss as many of them as you can.

Interpretation. You can expand on each reason in this way:

a. How does the Deuteronomic principle work in practice? Is it still in effect today? How has Jesus' death and resurrection affected the way this principle works in our lives?

b. Give some examples of the things that made Israel seem wise and understanding when compared with its neighbors. (See 4:6-8 and the box "Other Ancient Near Eastern Law Codes" on page 65.)

Note: The Deuteronomic principle sounds automatic, mechanical, materialistic. It may even sound like a principle of *earning* God's blessing. Later lessons in this study will show that we are able to obey God only by grace. For now, discuss why this principle, which would have been a blessing for sinless people, became a "law of sin and death" in practice. Refer to Romans 7 if necessary. Also, consider whether the effects of this principle are always immediate, material blessings or sufferings.

Application. You can ask questions like these about each reason for obedience: (1) Is this still a reason for us today? (2) If so, in what way is it still relevant? (3) If not, why not? (4) Can we learn anything about God's character or Jesus' work from this reason? The "For Further Study" question on page 62 may help you answer question 13, but expect some disagreement.

Then give everyone a chance to think over what they've learned and consider what they want to take to heart. Ask at least one person to describe one specific, measurable way he or she plans to apply something from 4:1-43. For example, regarding 4:16-20 a woman might say, "I tend to make an idol of my house. I'm much more likely to spend time working on it than serving the Lord. So, I'm going to make a list of all the reasons why the Lord, not my house, is my first priority and should run my life. For the next week, I'm going to see to it that I take fifteen minutes each day alone with God and thirty minutes a day listening to and loving my kids, even if this gets in the way of a clean house. I'm going to ask the Lord to enable me to do these things joyfully and to deliver me from Deuteronomy 4:28. I'm going to tape that verse to my refrigerator and vacuum cleaner so I will see it whenever I start to cook or clean.

Prayer. Thank God for His character as revealed in Deuteronomy 4. Thank Him for freedom through Christ from the Deuteronomic principle's curses. Ask Him for the grace to obey Him and to take to heart the motives you have studied.

Other Ancient Near Eastern Law Codes

Moses said, "What other nation is so great as to have such righteous decrees and laws as this body of laws I am setting before you today?" (Deuteronomy 4:8). A comparison with other Near Eastern nations shows that Moses spoke truly.

In centuries of history, Egypt never had a law code that gave predictable, consistent guidelines for rights, duties, and penalties. Indeed, the Egyptian language had no word for "law." The Pharaoh was regarded as a god on earth, whose every decree supposedly embodied truth and justice. It didn't matter whether people were treated alike or in proportion to their deeds. In the same way, the petty kings of ancient Palestine and Syria decided justice by their personal views, not by permanent laws.

(continued on page 66)

(continued from page 65)

We know of several Babylonian law codes: those of Ur, Lupit-Ishtar, and Hammurabi. However, none of these stated what judges were supposed to do. They recorded only what some judges had done in the past, so that a judge might use a case as a guide if he chose to do so. Assyria, likewise, compiled past decisions but left judges free to judge by their opinions.[3]

No other code than Israel's included religious law or claimed that a god gave it or was its authority for justice. No other code gave motives or reasons for its decisions, as in Deuteronomy 22:24, Exodus 20:5, and Exodus 23:8-9, for instance. Israel's Law commanded the death penalty for crimes against God and against the holiness of life, but it was strikingly humane compared to other codes. Only Deuteronomy 25:11-12 mentioned bodily mutilation, in contrast to many places in Babylonian, Hittite, and other codes. Flogging was limited to forty lashes (see Deuteronomy 25:3).

Other codes treated commoners' lives as less valuable than noblemen's. They regarded harm to a woman, a slave, or an ox all as harm to a man's property. For instance, if a nobleman caused the death of a noblewoman, Hammurabi's code said that the killer's *daughter* had to die. If a nobleman caused a slavewoman's death, he paid one third of a mina of silver to her owner.[4] By contrast, Israel's law protected women and slaves explicitly from being used as property and made justice the same for all social classes.

1. J. A. Thompson, Deuteronomy: *An Introduction and Commentary* (London: InterVarsity, 1974), 102.
2. Peter C. Craigie, *The Book of Deuteronomy* (Grand Rapids, MI: Eerdmans, 1976), 138; Thompson, 107.
3. Roland de Vaux, *Ancient Israel*, vol. 1 (New York: McGraw-Hill, 1965), 144–150.
4. Gordon Fee and Douglas Stuart, *How to Read the Bible for All Its Worth* (Grand Rapids, MI: Zondervan, 1982), 144.

DEUTERONOMY 4:44–6:25

Love God

*"Hear, O Israel: The LORD our God, the Lord is one.
Love the LORD your God with all your heart and
with all your soul and with all your strength."*
Deuteronomy 6:4-5

We hear a lot about love. It has even been said
that the Old Testament is about justice and the
New Testament is about love. But Moses told
the Israelites to put love at the center of their
relationship with the Lord, and he told them what
love meant. When Jesus talks about love in the New
Testament, He means the same thing.

Read 4:44–6:25 at least once before beginning
the questions. Ask God to show you what He is like
and what He desires from you through this passage.

1. Make up a title or short sentence that
   summarizes what each paragraph in this
   passage is about. (Feel free to make more or
   fewer divisions.)

   4:44-49 Introduces Moses' second speech,

   which extends through 28:68. These six verses

   summarize the prologue of chapters 103.

   5:1-21 _____

   _____

   5:22-33 _____

   _____

   6:1-3 _____

   _____

For Thought and Discussion: Most of the people who are hearing Moses' speech in Moab were either children or unborn when God made the covenant at Sinai. Therefore, what do you think Moses means in 5:2-3?

6:4-9 _____

_____

_____

6:10-19 _____

_____

_____

6:20-25 _____

_____

Fear the Lord

Not with our fathers . . . but with us (5:3). Of all the Israelites over twenty years old at the time of the Sinai (Horeb) covenant, only Moses, Joshua, and Caleb are still alive. The rest of this generation who made the covenant has died (see Numbers 14:28-35; Deuteronomy 2:14-16).

2. a. Observe how God revealed Himself to the Israelites at Sinai/Horeb (see 5:4-5,22-23). What attitude toward God did this experience produce in the people (see 5:5,23-27)?

_____

_____

_____

_____

_____

_____

_____

_____

b. Why did God approve of this attitude toward Him (see 5:28-29, 6:1-2)?

_____

_____

_____

_____

_____

_____

c. To what extent is this attitude appropriate for Christians? Why do you think so? (*Optional*: See Ephesians 3:11-12; Hebrews 10:19-31; 12:18-29; 1 Peter 1:17; 2:17; 1 John 4:17-18.)

_____

_____

_____

_____

_____

_____

_____

Love the Lord

Hearts (6:6). For a Hebrew, the heart was the seat of intellect, will, and emotions, the deep mind and core of a person.[1]

3. a. What do you think God meant by commanding that His commandments should be "upon your hearts" (6:6)?

_____

_____

Meditate on 6:1-9.
What responsibilities
do these verses
suggest you have
toward your children?
How can you
better fulfill those
responsibilities?
(Discuss at least one
specific way with your
spouse.)

**For Thought and
Discussion:** Why
might the sin of 6:10-
12 be an easy error to
fall into?

_____

_____

_____

_____

_____

b. Why is this important?

_____

_____

_____

_____

_____

_____

_____

_____

4. Against what sin did God warn the people in
6:10-12? (Describe it in your own words.)

_____

_____

_____

_____

Hear, O Israel (5:1; 6:3-4; 9:1; 20:3). Moses said this
repeatedly. Deuteronomy 6:4-9 was so central
to the covenant faith that it became part of the
prayers Israelites received daily. Orthodox Jews
still do this.[2]

5. a. What did Jesus say about Deuteronomy 6:4-5
in Matthew 22:34-40?

_____

_____

_____

_____

_____

_____

_____

_____

b. How should Jesus' words lead us to regard this Old Testament command?

_____

_____

_____

_____

6. Examine the confession (creed, statement of faith) in 6:4 closely, noting each word. What truths about the Lord are central to Israel's faith? (For example, "the LORD our God" implies that . . .)

_____

_____

_____

_____

_____

_____

_____

7. Deuteronomy 6:5 is the response we should make if we believe 6:4. This "greatest commandment" summarizes the first four

of the Ten Commandments, which the Lord gave at Sinai (see Exodus 20:1-17) and reaffirmed in Moab (see Deuteronomy 5:6-21). Look at Deuteronomy 5:6-15. In the following chart, state each command and explain how it is an aspect of love for God.

Command	How it shows our love for God
5:7	
5:8-10	
5:11	
5:12-15	

Misuse the name (5:11). Ancient people believed that a person's or a god's name had power and might be invoked for a magical curse or manipulation. A god's name also had authority for prayer or to justify a war or enterprise. The Hebrew for "misuse" means "vanity" or "worthless purpose."[3] Thus, to misuse God's name would be to invoke it in magic, prayer, or planning for some end He has not authorized.

8. The command in 5:8-10 has two facets. On the one hand, we must not worship idols of other gods. On the other hand, we must not make images of the Lord to worship because He is beyond all images we might make (see 4:15-19). Give one example each of how a Christian might . . .

idolize something or someone other than the Lord and worship it alongside Him

_____

_____

_____

_____

_____

_____

_____

worship an image of the Lord rather than the Holy One Himself

_____

_____

_____

_____

_____

_____

Optional Application: How can you cultivate a love for the Lord that allows no other audience or pursuit to take priority? What gets in the way of your love for Him? You might take this issue to Him in prayer, as in Psalm 86:11 and 139:23-24.

Optional Application: Do you ever pray for or do something without asking God whether it has worth in His eyes (see 5:11)? If so, how can you avoid doing this?

For Further Study:
List all the signs of
God's love in 1:1–4:43.

**For Thought and
Discussion:** Think
about each of the
commands in 6:13
("fear," "serve," "take
your oaths"). How
does each relate to
love?

9. Our love for God is a response to His nature (see
6:4) and character. What signs of God's love for
us do you see in 5:6-15 and 6:10-12?

_____

_____

_____

_____

_____

_____

Heart . . . soul . . . strength (6:5). These were not
thought of as distinct parts of a person. Hebrew
used parallelism for emphasis. The sense in
6:5-6 is to love with one's whole being.[4]

---

10. Many people today think that love is just a
feeling, yet God commands it.

a. Why can God rightly command us to have an
inner heart-attitude of love for Him? (Consider
question 9.)

_____

_____

_____

_____

b. How is love more than just an inner attitude
(see 5:6-15, 6:5)?

_____

_____

_____

_____

_____

_____

The Torah today

Study Skill—Application

Here are some of the most frequent obstacles to applying God's Word:

1. "I didn't have time to meditate on and pray about passages this week." Answer: What do you think about while in the car, getting dressed, or doing other things besides working and talking? Most people have at least a few minutes a day in which they can think about God rather than earthly concerns. Try turning off the radio and television and just being quiet or noisy with God.

2. "I forget to think about Scripture during my free moments." Make reminders: Tape a card with a reminder or quotation to your dashboard, refrigerator, desk, or mirror. Tie a string on your finger, purse, or briefcase. Try any gimmick that helps!

3. "I pray, study, and meditate every morning, but I forget about it during the day." Again, put reminders in your house, car, office, and so on. It's important to let the Scripture come to mind frequently during the day.

4. "I can't ever think of specific ways to act on what the Scripture says." Divide your life into spheres (home, work, church, school) or people (spouse, children, coworkers, boss, church friends). Choose one person and pray about what that person needs from you, what might prevent you from fulfilling that need, and how you might fulfill that need. Or review a recent situation in which you sinned. Look for a similar situation in the near future to act rightly. Ask God to enable you to recognize and respond rightly to the situation.

Persistent prayer, inviting God to show you opportunities to apply what you have learned, will be answered.

For Further Study:
The "test" (6:16) at Massah in the wilderness was a demand that the Lord prove His power and love by providing water for the people (see Exodus 17:7). How is the sin of testing related to the sins of making images (see Deuteronomy 5:8) and misusing the Lord's name (see 5:11)?

Optional Application:
Meditate this week on one of the commandments or on 6:4-5. Look for ways that you can live up to these commands better.

11. a. What implications does this lesson have for the way you treat God?

_____

_____

_____

_____

_____

_____

_____

_____

_____

b. How can you put one of those implications into practice in some way this week?

_____

_____

_____

_____

_____

_____

_____

12. List any questions you have about the material in this lesson.

_____

_____

_____

_____

_____

For the group

Warm-up. The Lord says a great deal about *parents* (especially fathers) and *children* in this section (5:3,9-10,14,16; 6:2-3,7,10,20-25). Passing on knowledge of the Lord seems to be central. You might begin your meeting by asking members to share one thing—true or false, good or bad—they learned about the Lord from their parents. Or ask members to share what they learned about love from their parents.

Observation. You might focus your discussion on what it means to love the Lord. First, observe what the passage says about His character and acts toward Israel. Next, observe what the passage says about loving Him (see 5:6-15; 6:1-19). Together, list everything you notice.

Interpretation. Now try to define what love means. Then go back and discuss how each command in 5:6-15 and 6:1-19 shows love for God. Clarify what each command means. Finally, refine your definition or description of love.

Question 6 asks you to draw out the significance of 6:4. Your list should include such statements as "The Lord is our God—the only object of our worship, the supreme authority of our lives. The Lord is one God, not many gods as pagans worship." The Church of Jesus Christ of Latter Day Saints (Mormons) teaches that the Lord is one of a hierarchy of gods—is this biblical faith? Also, how does Deuteronomy 6:4 fit with the Christian doctrine of the Trinity? (It does, but how?) These are just a few of the issues that 6:4 raises.

Application. First make sure that everyone understands why and how the Ten Commandments apply to Christians. It may be hard at first to see how idolatry is a danger to Christians, but discuss how each command in 5:6-15, 6:4-5, and 6:10-12 applies to you. Again, give everyone a chance to share how he intends to let something in this lesson affect his own life. For more guidance on applying the Old Testament, refer the group to the box "Law and Grace" on page 78.

Prayer. Praise God for His nature (see 5:6,9-10; 6:4). Ask Him to reveal Himself more and more to you and to help you love Him as He deserves to be loved.

Law and Grace

Jesus calls Deuteronomy 6:5 "the first and greatest commandment" and Leviticus 19:18 "the second" (Matthew 22:34-40). He gives us a "new command" (John 13:34): "Love each other as I have loved you" (John 15:12). By obeying this command, we show our love for the Lord and receive His love (see John 14:15; 15:9).

Paul tells us that God put our sinful nature to death on the cross "in order that the righteous requirements of the law might be fully met in us, who do not live according to the sinful nature but according to the Spirit" (Romans 8:3-4; compare 8:29). What are those righteous requirements that reflect the character of Jesus in us? Paul says,

> The commandments, "Do not commit adultery," "Do not murder," "Do not steal," "Do not covet," and whatever other commandment there may be, are summed up in the one rule: "Love your neighbor as yourself." Love does no harm to its neighbor. Therefore, love is the fulfillment of the law. (Romans 13:9-10)

Jesus also points us to the Ten Commandments in Matthew 5:17–6:34 and 15:1-9. Much of His Sermon on the Mount and other teaching is commentary on the Ten Commandments; rightly understood, the Decalogue ("ten words") tells us how to love God and our neighbor.

However, there is a difference between the ways of obedience under the old and new covenants. Paul explains that Jesus' death enables us to do what the Law could not: obey by the power of the Holy Spirit living in us (see Romans 7:4-6; 8:4-13). Paul stresses that in order to please God and become like Christ, we must rely utterly on God's grace to forgive our failures and empower our successes (see 2 Corinthians 4:7; 12:7-10; Philippians 3:4-11).

The absolute necessity of grace shapes how we apply Old Testament teaching. First, we should always ask the Lord what passage He wants us to apply and how He wants us to apply it. Proverbs 3:5-6 encourages us to depend upon God for all guidance. We may not hear a voice dictating a specific application, but the attitude of humble dependence is essential. It keeps us from doing as we please and getting nowhere.

Second, we should always ask God for the ability to do what He asks (see Ephesians 3:14-21; Galatians 3:3). If He has guided us to this application, He will provide the ability. Application by our power and design is as bad as no application; it is like the Israelites' attack that God had forbidden (see Deuteronomy 1:41-46).

Third, we should be ready to fail, confess, and repent frequently when we are growing (see 1 John 1:8-10). The Lord does not give us immediate success, lest we feel proud of ourselves.

1. Peter C. Craigie, *The Book of Deuteronomy* (Grand Rapids, MI: Eerdmans, 1976), 170; J. A. Thompson, *Deuteronomy: An Introduction and Commentary* (London: InterVarsity, 1974), 122.
2. J. A. Thompson, *Deuteronomy: An Introduction and Commentary* (London: InterVarsity, 1974), 121.
3. Craigie, 155–156.
4. Craigie, 170.

LESSON SIX

DEUTERONOMY 5:16-21; 6:20-25

Law and Faith

"Love your neighbor as yourself. I am the LORD."
Leviticus 19:18

Whatever our political leanings, Christians believe in upholding legitimate human rights. But what are those rights, according to God? The New Testament affirms that the Ten Commandments are still God's definition of how human beings should be treated.

The Law, and the Ten Commandments in particular, is fundamentally a guide to *justice*; it explains what we owe to others. It tells what our *duties* are to God and people; put differently, it states what rights God and people can justly expect from others.[1] Deuteronomy 5:7-15 and 6:4-5 define God's rights, and 5:16-21 defines human rights. Chapters 12–26 explain some implications of these rights.

According to Jesus, Leviticus 19:18 summarizes man's duty to man (see Matthew 22:39-40). In Romans 13:7-10, Paul explains that "love is the fulfillment of the law" of the Ten Commandments.

Reread Deuteronomy 5:16-21 and 6:20-25. Think about the relationship between God and Israel that lies behind the Ten Commandments. Think about what *justice* and *love* each mean.

For Further Study: Compare Matthew 22:39-40 to John 15:12-13. How does Jesus' command go beyond justice, beyond loving our neighbor as ourself? (See also Matthew 5:43-48, Luke 6:27-36.)

Love your neighbor (5:16-21)

1. The apostle Paul observed that Deuteronomy 5:16 is "the first commandment with a promise" (Ephesians 6:1-3). Why do you suppose God

81

links long life and prosperity especially with honoring parents?

_____

_____

_____

_____

_____

_____

_____

2. How does Deuteronomy 5:16 apply to Christian . . .

minor children (see Ephesians 6:1-2)?

_____

_____

_____

_____

_____

adults (Matthew 15:1-9 suggests one way)?

_____

_____

_____

_____

_____

_____

_____

Murder (5:17). Private killing. War and judicial executions (such as for idolatry and murder) were lawful under stated circumstances.

3. For each of the last five commandments, read the New Testament cross-references. Then write some ways each commandment teaches us to love our neighbors. Look for positive things to do as well as negative things to avoid.

Deuteronomy 5:17 (Matthew 5:21-24)

I must avoid and repent of all anger, bitterness, and

unforgiveness. I should seek to enhance my neighbor's

life by . . .

_____

_____

_____

Deuteronomy 5:18 (Matthew 5:27-32; Ephesians 5:21-33)

_____

_____

_____

_____

_____

_____

_____

Deuteronomy 5:19 (Luke 6:29-38; 2 Corinthians 9:6-11; Ephesians 4:28)

_____

_____

_____

_____

For Thought and Discussion: Some people think the Old Testament Law was concerned only with outward behavior and that Jesus changed it to demand pure inner motives. Do the Ten Commandments support this claim? Explain your view.

**Optional
Application:** How
can you enhance your
neighbor's life? Honor
your parents? Act
upon one of the other
commandments?

Deuteronomy 5:20 (Matthew 5:33-37; Luke
21:12-19; Ephesians 4:25,29,31)

_____

_____

_____

_____

_____

Deuteronomy 5:21 (Luke 12:13-34; 16:13;
Philippians 4:11-13)

_____

_____

_____

_____

_____

4. How can you actively love your neighbor in
   one of the ways you just named? Think of some
   specific steps you can take.

_____

_____

_____

_____

_____

_____

_____

Righteousness (6:20-25)

Deuteronomy 6:20-25 is another creed (a confession of faith) that Jews have memorized for centuries.

Righteousness (6:25). "True and personal relationship with the covenant God."[2] The covenant defines the relationship between God and man, so to keep the covenant requirements is to maintain the relationship.

　　For some of the covenant requirements not detailed in Deuteronomy, see the box "Sacrifice: Old Testament Grace" on page 90.

---

5. When a son asks the significance of the commandments, a father should answer with a summary of Israel's faith (see 6:20-25). What aspects of that faith focus on God's acts of grace (unearned kindness) (see 6:20-23)?

_____

_____

_____

_____

_____

_____

6. How does Israel maintain a righteous relationship to God (see 6:24-25)?

_____

_____

_____

_____

_____

_____

For Thought and Discussion: According to 5:9-10, what happens to descendants of people who rebel against God? How does Jesus' death free us from the effects of this law?

85

The Torah today

7. Compare Deuteronomy 6:20-25 to Romans 3:22-24; Philippians 3:4-9; and 1 John 1:8-10.

   a. How do Christians obtain and maintain a right relationship to God under the new covenant?

   obtain _____

   _____

   _____

   maintain _____

   _____

   _____

   b. How is this like and unlike the system under the old covenant?

   _____

   _____

   _____

   _____

   _____

   _____

8. a. Like Israel, Christians express their righteous relationship to God by active obedience (see John 14:15; 15:9-14). However, what happens when we try to keep the commands by our own strength (see Romans 7:14-25)?

   _____

   _____

   _____

   _____

   _____

b. Therefore, how is it possible for us to keep God's commands (see John 15:4-6; Romans 8:1-14; Galatians 3:1-5; 5:16-18)?

_____

_____

_____

_____

_____

_____

c. How are our resources different from those available to Israel?

_____

_____

_____

_____

_____

_____

9. In question 4, you wrote one way in which you can actively love your neighbor. How should your answers to questions 5–8 affect the way you obey this command?

_____

_____

_____

_____

_____

_____

_____

For Thought and Discussion: What should we do if we fail when we try to apply what the Lord is saying to us in Scripture (see Philippians 3:12-14; 1 John 1:9)?

10. (*Optional*) Summarize what you have learned so far about the similarities and differences between the old and new covenants.

similarities _____

_____

_____

_____

_____

_____

differences _____

_____

_____

_____

_____

11. (*Optional*) Reread 6:20-25. Then write your own confession of faith—what you might tell your son if he asked you, "Why do we try to love God and our neighbors?"

_____

_____

_____

_____

_____

12. List any questions you have about this lesson.

_____

_____

_____

For the group

Warm-up. Moses said, "If we are careful to obey . . . that will be our righteousness" (6:25). In other words, we will be in right, intimate, Father-child, Lord-servant relationship with God if we do what He tells us. This lesson easily convinces us that we can earn God's love by doing right and His rejection by doing wrong. For some of us, this is a deeply ingrained error.

You might begin by letting each person share how he and his parents treated rules when he was a child. For instance, did he scrupulously try to obey, or was he always in trouble? Did his parents punish severely, discipline carefully, or permit everything? Did they hug and give affection after discipline? How did he feel about this treatment? Don't take more than a minute or two apiece for this; just let everyone express how he or she was trained to feel about rules.

Observation/Interpretation. This lessons breaks into two parts. The first deals with the commands in 5:16-21, and the second with the creed in 6:20-25.

a. You might devote five minutes apiece to discussing each of the six commandments in 5:16-21. What does each tell you about God's priorities? About loving your neighbor? About justice? What is Jesus' attitude toward each commandment in the Gospels?

Jesus points out that keeping the commandments goes beyond the letter of the Law. How far do you think He would go? For instance, does "You shall not murder" include actively supporting the enhancement of others' lives? Or what is the opposite of coveting others' possessions?

b. Next, what are the important points of Israel's faith as expressed in 6:20-25? What is the role of grace in that faith? The role of works? How is the Christian faith similar and different?

Application. Try brainstorming ways you could better fulfill the commandments. (This should take at least half your discussion time.) Take each command in turn. For instance, list ways in which adult Christians can honor their parents in thought and action. When you have listed as many ideas as you can think of, go back and discuss practical ways you can apply one or two of them to yourselves. (For instance, do you have whole, honoring thoughts toward, and relations with, your parents?) Then turn to the next command.

You might each choose one commandment to meditate on and to try to keep better. In doing so, think about how the old covenant faith of 6:20-25 does and doesn't apply to you.

Try question 11 together orally. What beliefs about God and Christ motivate you to obey God's words?

Prayer. Some people may feel moved to confess failure to keep the commandments as they should. Some may want to thank God for His commandments and for enabling us to be righteous in His eyes despite our failure to keep the commandments. You can also ask God for the grace to keep His commandments better than you have.

Sacrifice: Old Testament Grace

Moses told the Israelites that if they obeyed all the laws God gave them, God would declare them righteous (see Deuteronomy 6:25). God knew they were unable to obey perfectly, not because the laws were unreasonable but because the people were rebellious by nature. However, His own righteous character demanded that He answer every act of disobedience with just penalties. Yet God knew that if He made the people bear the just consequences of all their deeds, they would be dead in days or weeks. As Romans 6:23 explains, "The wages of sin is death."

Therefore, in order to be perfectly just but also loving and merciful, the Lord instituted the system of sacrifices detailed in the book of Leviticus. The basic principle behind the system was *substitution*; an animal died in place of the sinful person in order to restore fellowship between the person and God. The animal bore the death penalty for the person. There were five main kinds of sacrifices:

1. *Burnt offering.* A whole animal without defect was burned. This was a voluntary act of worship by an individual and was also offered twice daily for the whole nation. It atoned for (covered, paid for) unintentional sin in general. It expressed "devotion, commitment, and complete surrender to God" (see Leviticus 1:1-17; 6:8-13; 8:18-21; 16:24).

2. *Grain offering.* Along with a drink offering, this accompanied the burnt and fellowship offerings. It could include grain, fine flour, baked bread, olive oil, incense, and salt. Yeast and honey were forbidden. This was a "recognition of God's goodness and provisions" (see Leviticus 2:1-16; 6:14-23).

3. *Fellowship offering.* "Peace offering" in KJV. Part of the animal and bread was burned (for God), part was eaten by the priests, and part was eaten by the offerers. This was the only offering of which the offerer ate a part. It was a communal meal to celebrate and give thanks for peace and fellowship among offerers, priests, and God (see Leviticus 3:1-17; 7:11-34).

4. *Sin offering.* An animal (or fine flour if the offerer was very poor) was burned. The offerer laid his hands on the animal to identify with it, transferring his sins. Then the substitute was slaughtered. Most of the animal was burned outside the camp at the ceremonial ash heap, rather than on the altar, because the animal carried sin. The sin offering was required atonement for a specific unintentional sin, and the slaughtering represented forgiveness and cleansing (see Leviticus 4:1–5:13; 6:24-30; 8:14-17; 16:3-22).

5. *Guilt offering.* "Trespass offering" in KJV. This was like the sin offering but used in cases where restitution was possible (and therefore required), such as theft and cheating. The repentant sinner brought a ram to be slaughtered, made restitution for the sin, and paid the aggrieved person twenty percent extra (see Leviticus 5:14–6:7; 7:1-6).

When more than one kind of offering was presented, the sequence was usually *sin or guilt offering* (sin had to be dealt with first), *burnt offering* (commitment to God came next), *fellowship and grain offerings* (peace and fellowship were at last celebrated).[3]

(continued on page 92)

(continued from page 91)

In addition to these sacrifices, the annual Day of Atonement dealt with any unintentional sins of which people were unaware. One goat was killed as a sin offering, and one was chased into the desert after the priest put all the nation's sins onto the goat's head (see Leviticus 16:1-34).[4]

When you read laws like the Ten Commandments and God's repeated demands for perfect obedience, remember that from the outset, God provided for continual failure, atonement, and forgiveness. The gracious cleansing, forgiveness, and fellowship of the sacrificial system foreshadowed Christ's death (see Hebrews 9:1–10:39).

1. E. Calvin Beisner, "Equal Rights But . . ." *Discipleship Journal* 21 (May 1984), 39–42.
2. Peter C. Craigie, *The Book of Deuteronomy* (Grand Rapids, MI: Eerdmans, 1976), 175.
3. Kenneth Barker, ed., *The NIV Study Bible* (Grand Rapids, MI: Zondervan, 1985), 147–155.
4. Scripture specifies sin and guilt offerings for cases of unintentional sin (see Leviticus 4:2; 5:15), but many people assume that these offerings were also made when someone sinned intentionally but repented. The laws of the Day of Atonement do not mention *unintentional* sin, so that ceremony may have covered intentional sins committed during the previous year.

DEUTERONOMY 7:1-26

Holiness

"You are a people holy to the Lord your God."
Deuteronomy 7:6

God has sent us as Christians into the world with a crucial, glorious mission: to proclaim His salvation by word and deed. It is a spiritual war that we fight by unearthly means.

Israel, too, had a mission, a war to fight, a kingdom to conquer in God's name. Moses would not be with the warriors when they faced the Enemy, but he gave them truths about God to remember when the long struggle assailed them with temptations.

Read 7:1-26, looking for its central message.

1. a. What title would you give to 7:1-26?

   _____

   _____

   b. Divide the chapter into paragraphs and give each a title. Then compare your chapter title to the one on page 16, and your paragraph titles to the subtitles in this lesson.

   _____

   _____

   _____

   _____

   _____

For Thought and Discussion: How are the foes and tactics of Christian spiritual warfare like and unlike those of ancient Israel's war (see Romans 12:17-21; 2 Corinthians 6:14; 10:3-6; Ephesians 6:10-18)?

93

_____

_____

_____

_____

Destruction (7:1-6,25-26)

Sacred stones . . . Asherah poles . . . idols (7:5). Archaeologists have found Canaanite shrines to which a stone pillar stands beside the altar to represent the god Baal. A hole for a wooden post, a symbol of the goddess Asherah, is in the ground nearby. Idols, symbols of carved stone, have also been found.[1]

  For more on this subject, see "Canaanite Religion" on pages 100–101.

2. How did God command the Israelites to treat the people they conquered in the Promised Land (see 7:1-3)?

_____

_____

_____

_____

_____

3. What were they supposed to do with the Canaanite's religious objects (see 7:5,25-26)?

_____

_____

_____

_____

4. Why did God command this treatment?

  7:4,16 _____

_____

_____

_____

7:6 _____

_____

_____

_____

For Further Study: Do a word study on *holy* and *holiness* in the Old Testament. Look the words up first in a Bible dictionary or go directly to a concordance. The concordance will point you to all the places in the Old Testament that use these words. Write down what you observe: Who or what is holy? What makes them holy? What are the implications of being holy? You might want to start with just five references. See page 217 for more on concordances.

Treaty (7:2). The Hebrew word is *b'rith*, the same word as "covenant" in 7:9. Consider what making a covenant/treaty with the Canaanites would have done to Israel's covenant/treaty with the Sovereign Lord.

Holy (7:6). Utterly set apart for God from common use or service. The Canaanites also regarded their gods as "holy," but to them holiness was simply the awesome quality of supernatural beings. By contrast, the holiness of Israel's Lord included moral perfection as well as awe-inspiring transcendence.[2]

For Thought and Discussion: Do you think 7:26 applies to keeping non-Christian religious images as artwork in a Christian home? Why or why not?

5. Why did Israel's special status as "holy" and God's treasured possession" (7:6) demand the drastic action of 7:1-5?

_____

_____

_____

_____

6. Christians, too, are holy to the Lord (see 1 Peter 1:15-16; 2:9). Does 7:1-5,26 have any application for our lives? If so, how does it apply? If not, why not?

_____

_____

_____

_____

_____

_____

_____

Covenant love (7:7-16)

7. Why did God choose Israel to be His treasured possession, holy to Himself (see 7:7-8; 10:14-15)?

_____

_____

_____

_____

_____

_____

8. The people did not earn their election either by their innate greatness (see 7:7) or moral excellence (see 9:4-6). What does 7:7-8 tell you about God's eternal character?

_____

_____

_____

_____

_____

9. Write down everything you observe in 7:9-10 about the Lord's character and attributes.

_____

_____

_____

_____

_____

_____

_____

_____

_____

For Further Study: To expand Deuteronomy 7:9-10, compare Exodus 33:18–34:14 and Isaiah 6:1-7.

For Further Study: How does God show love for His people (see 7:12-15)? Notice the Deuteronomic principle again.

10. How should these truths about God affect our attitudes (toward self, God, things, priorities, and so on) and actions?

_____

_____

_____

_____

_____

_____

_____

Courage (7:14-24)

11. The Israelites might have doubted their ability to conquer the Promised Land (see 7:17). What facts about God did Moses recount to encourage the people?

7:18-19 _____

_____

_____

_____

7:20,23-24 _____

For Thought and Discussion: Why did God not drive out Israel's enemies all at once (see 7:22)? Does this principle operate in the life of a Christian? If so, how?

Optional Application: How does 7:17-24 encourage you to face what God asks of you?

7:21 _____

_____

_____

_____

12. What differences do the facts about God in 7:17-24 make to your life?

_____

_____

_____

_____

_____

The Torah today

13. Questions 6, 10, and 12 all suggest possible ways to apply 7:1-26. Choose one area of your life and describe how you can let one aspect of 7:1-26 affect your thoughts, decisions, and actions this week.

_____

_____

_____

_____

_____

_____

_____

_____

14. List your questions about chapter 7.

_____

_____

_____

_____

For the group

Warm-up. Ask everyone to think of a time when he or she was chosen to do something. Then give everyone a chance to describe how it felt to be chosen.

Questions. This lesson emphasizes God's character, which is the same now as it was in Moses' day. A secondary theme is the Holy War to destroy the idolaters and conquer Canaan. Because we must be wary in extracting universal principles from that unique part of God's plan, you may prefer to focus on God's character, which is easier to apply to the Christian life.

If the terminology in question 9 confuses your group, explain that God's *character* means His love, justice, mercy, the way He treats people, what He values, and so on. His *attributes* are His power, divinity, holiness, wisdom, and so on.

Many people find the concept of the Holy War confusing because modern religious groups justify their own wars by claiming to fight by God's command. Anyone who claims this falsely is grossly misusing God's name (see 5:11). Christians should recognize that many groups who profess to be fighting holy wars are sincere, but sincerely wrong. This should make us wary of making the claim for ourselves. We need to pray earnestly for discernment and humility for ourselves and others. However, the fact that many people abuse God's authority does not mean that He did not authorize Israel's battles.

The New Testament says a great deal about spiritual warfare but little about physical warfare. This does not of itself rule out Christian involvement in physical warfare, but it does suggest that we should study Deuteronomy more for principles that apply to our spiritual war than for tactics for physical war. Christians have been discussing the legitimacy of physical war for almost two thousand years; if you are interested, ask your pastor to refer you to books that address all sides of this issue.

Evaluation. It is a good idea to evaluate your study after a few weeks so that you can improve it for the future. Here are two approaches to evaluation; you can select from both if you prefer.

1. Look at the goals you set at the beginning of this study. Are you doing the best you can to meet them? (For instance, in what ways are you getting to know God and each other better? Is the study encouraging you to grow more like Christ or to know and act on the Bible better? If not, what is lacking, and how can you improve the study?)

2. Ask the group these three simple (but perhaps too general) questions:
- What did you like best about this meeting?
- What did you like least?
- How could this study be changed to meet your needs better?

Prayer. Praise God for His character as revealed in chapter 7. Ask Him to enable you to believe and act on your knowledge of Him as you fight your spiritual battles.

Canaanite Religion, Part 1

From recorded myths, inscriptions, and references in the Old Testament, we know a little about Canaanite religion. First, the Canaanites did not believe that one Person or Power created the world and was in charge of nature and human religions. Instead, they thought that myriad *baalim* and *elohim* (lords, geniuses, deities, spirits) governed sun, rain, harvest, animal fertility, the planets, and so on.

All these "holy ones" belonged to a clan.

El—the gods' father and the world's creator—had reputedly delegated control of the world to his sons and daughters, so although he was formally acknowledged, he received little worship. His son *Baal*, lord of the sky and rains, was much more involved in human affairs. Humans could solicit his favor by feeding him with sacrifices and performing magical rituals.

Three goddesses, or three faces of one goddess, were also highly esteemed in Canaan. The Mother, *Asherah*, ruled the home; *Ashtoreth* (*Astarte*), the Lover, ruled fertility; and the Virgin, *Anath*, ruled war and hunting. They were also seen as virgin-mother-crone, birth-life-death, the new-full-old moon, and other magical trinities. (Exact beliefs about each goddess varied from city to city; for example, some Canaanite myths show Anath as goddess of love and sexuality as well as war. Concepts of the triple goddess overlapped in the Near East.

Other deities abounded. Dagon (Corn) was "genius of the crops." Sun and Moon, Dawn and Sunset, Sea, and Death all had rituals. All were regarded as "holy," but the word meant chiefly "other, beyond human." The gods did not act according to any moral laws, nor were they interested in human goodness or justice. They supposedly could be persuaded to act for good or ill by flattery, begging, sacrifice, or magic. However, because they cared nothing for humans and had no morality, they were mysterious, unpredictable, and fearful. Personal intimacy and covenant love between human and god was out of the question.[3]

---

1. J. A. Thompson, *Deuteronomy: An Introduction and Commentary* (London: InterVarsity, 1974), 129.
2. Thompson, 130.
3. Theodore H. Gaster, "The Religion of the Canaanites," *Ancient Religions*, ed. Vergilius Ferm (New York: The Philosophical Library, 1950), 113–143; Walter Beyerlin, ed., *Near Eastern Religious Texts Relating to the Old Testament* (Philadelphia: Westminster, 1978), 185–268; J. I. Packer, Merrill C. Tenney, William White Jr. *The World of the Old Testament* (Nashville: Nelson, 1982), 1973–180.

LESSON EIGHT

DEUTERONOMY 9:1–10:11

Pride

---

*"Understand, then, that it is not because of your
righteousness that the LORD your God is giving you
this good land to possess, for you are a stiff-necked
people."*

Deuteronomy 9:6

Christians walk a thin line. We may get lost in the
world around us if we forget that we are called to be
special and sent to fulfill a crucial, glorious mission.
Or, if we remember our calling and mission, we may
feel superior to others who know God less well than
we do. Somehow it's hard to keep a clear, balanced
view of our identity.

Israel had this problem. In chapter 7 of
Deuteronomy, Moses warned Israel not to assimilate
with pagan neighbors by conforming to their ways.
Now, in chapter 9, he cautions the people also to
avoid misplaced pride in their separateness. Read
9:1–10:11.

1. Write a title for 9:1–10:11 and subtitles for each
   paragraph.

   _____

   _____

   _____

   _____

   _____

   _____

   _____

   _____

103

For Thought and Discussion: Members of certain groups have at times claimed that God covenanted to give them land and dominion over the land's former inhabitants. How could a modern Christian verify or disprove such a claim?

Two stone tablets (9:10-11; 10:1). "In keeping with ancient Near Eastern practice, these were duplicates of the covenant document, not two sections of the Ten Commandments. One copy belonged to each party of the covenant. Since Israel's copy was to be laid up in the presence of her God (according to custom), both covenant tablets (God's and Israel's) were placed in the ark.[1]

The tablets were the "Testimony" (Exodus 31:18) or "covenant stipulations"[2] that told how the Israelites would show loyalty to their Sovereign.

Chest . . . ark (10:1-3). "Both words translate the same Hebrew word, which means 'chest' or 'box.' After initially translating 'chest' for clarity, the NIV reverts to the more traditional and familiar rendering 'ark.'"[3]

2. Because of their special status as "holy" and God's "treasured possession" (7:6), and because of their mission to destroy the wicked Canaanites (see 9:4), the Israelites were tempted to be proud. What were they inclined to believe about themselves (see 9:4)?

3. By contrast, on what basis was Israel in fact chosen to conquer Canaan?

104

7:8; 10:14-15 _____

_____

_____

_____

9:4 _____

_____

_____

_____

4. a. What attitude like the one in 9:4 might a
Christian be tempted to have?

_____

_____

_____

_____

b. How can a Christian resist this temptation?

_____

_____

_____

_____

5. To quell their pride, Moses also reminded the
people of the character they had displayed since
the flight from Egypt.
How did Moses describe the Israelites in
9:6-7?

_____

_____

_____

_____

**For Thought and
Discussion:** a. From
what you have read,
what gave Israel
the "right" to the
Promised Land?
What "rights" did the
Canaanites have?
b. How does this
situation affect your
notions of justice?
c. Do you think
this was a special
situation, or is it
relevant to modern
land disputes? Why or
why not?

**Optional
Application:** a.
Do Christians ever
resemble Israel in
9:6-7? Have you ever
been like that? If so,
how?
b. Ask God to
forgive you for this
attitude and change
you. Meditate on
9:6-7 this week and
ask God to show
you opportunities to
act in humility and
obedience.

105

How did the Israelites
show their stiff-
necked stubbornness
at Kadesh Barnea (see
1:26-46; 9:23)?

**For Thought and
Discussion:** What
do you learn about
leadership from
Moses' response to
God's anger at Israel
(see 9:18-21,25-29)?

6. How did they show these traits at Horeb (see
   9:8-12)?

   _____

   _____

   _____

   _____

   _____

7. a. How did God plan to respond to this behavior
      (see 9:13-14)?

   _____

   _____

   _____

   _____

   b. Why was He going to do this (see 4:24;
      7:9-10)?

   _____

   _____

   _____

   _____

   _____

8. God's justice and holiness required this response
   unless Moses did something. What did Moses
   do to prevent God from destroying Israel (see
   9:18-21,25-29)?

   _____

   _____

   _____

   _____

   _____

9. God's mercy enabled Him to forgive Israel when Moses did this (see 4:31). How do you think Moses' prayer let God be merciful without ceasing to be just and holy?

Optional Application: Specifically how can you avoid resembling the Israelites (see 9:7-24) in your response to God's grace?

_____

_____

_____

_____

_____

_____

The Torah today

10. a. How does Christ do for us what Moses did for Israel in Deuteronomy 9:18-21,25-29? (Compare Psalm 106:23 to Hebrews 7:25.)

_____

_____

_____

_____

_____

   b. What can Christians do to turn aside or soften God's judgment on their neighbors (see 2 Chronicles 7:14; James 5:16-20)?

_____

_____

_____

_____

_____

Optional Application: How might you begin acting on Moses' example in 9:18-21,25-29 with regard to your prayers for individuals or the church?

For Thought and Discussion: What does 9:1-29 reveal about God?

c. Why has God made the experiences of believers dependent upon the prayers and actions of others? (See, for example, 1 Corinthians 12:12,21; Ephesians 4:16.)

_____

_____

_____

_____

_____

_____

_____

11. a. Read question 4 and the "Optional Application" questions in this lesson. Is there one insight from 9:1–10:11 that you would like to act upon this week? If so, what is it?

_____

_____

_____

_____

_____

_____

b. What specific steps can you take to apply this insight?

_____

_____

_____

_____

_____

_____

108

12. List any questions you have about this lesson.

_____

_____

_____

_____

For the group

Warm-up. Have the group take a minute or two
to consider whether they have ever felt better than
non-Christians because of their relationship with
God.

Questions. This lesson deals with a moral issue and
a paradox about God. The moral issue is pride—we
scorn God's grace toward us when we imagine that
He has chosen us over unbelievers because we are
better. Draw attention to the fact that grace was the
basis of Israel's election, just as it is of ours. We need
to see that God continued to love the Israelites while
they were continually rebellious and stiff-necked.

The second matter is twofold. First, how do
God's holiness and justice, which require someone
to bear the consequences for sin, remain consistent with His love and mercy? Second, since God is
changeless and all-knowing, why does He command
us to pray and behave as though our prayers affect
His choices? You probably won't resolve this paradox, but you may learn a lot and be more motivated
to pray seriously.

Restating. In even the best study guide, a question
is occasionally unclear. Also, groups often find it
helpful and more interesting when leaders rephrase
the questions instead of just repeating them. So
when you want to restate a question, keep these
two sets of categories in mind: (1) the procedure of
observe-interpret-apply, and (2) the topics of "Who
is God?" "Who am I?" and "What should I do?"

For example, you can restate an observation like
this: "What does this verse [or paragraph] say about
God [His character, acts, and so on]?" Or "What
does this verse [or paragraph] say about man's
unredeemed nature or his nature/identity in Christ?"

**Optional
Application:** Are
there any verses that
you might memorize
and meditate on this
week? Consider 7:6,
7:9-10, 7:21, 7:22, 7:25-
26, 9:4, 9:5, 9:6, 9:21,
9:26-29, 10:14-16, or
some other passage
that strikes you.

109

Or "What does this paragraph say we should think or do?"

For interpretation, try asking, "How does this passage apply to you?" Or "What implications does this passage have for your life?" Or "What specific steps can you take to act on this teaching?"

Prayer. Thank God for His character as revealed in this passage. Ask Him to lead you away from pride and toward holiness, toward a sense of being His chosen, treasured people. Then you might practice interceding for the sins and needs of each other, your church, or your country.

1. Kenneth Barker, ed., *The NIV Study Bible* (Grand Rapids, MI: Zondervan, 1985), 133.
2 Barker, 123.
3. Barker, 258.

LESSON NINE

DEUTERONOMY 8:1-20; 10:12–11:32

Doubting God

"To the LORD your God belong the heavens, even the highest heavens, the earth and everything in it. Yet the LORD set his affection on your forefathers and loved them, and he chose you, their descendants, above all the nations, as it is today. Circumcise your hearts, therefore, and do not be stiff-necked any longer."
                    Deuteronomy 10:14-16

No matter how often God has been there when we needed Him, it's easy to doubt Him when the pressure is on. Moses wanted Israel to learn at least four lessons from their time in the wilderness, lessons to overcome four common doubts about Him.

Read Deuteronomy 7:1–11:32, skimming chapters 7, 9, and 11 and paying particular attention to chapters 8 and 10. Ask God to show you the lessons from Israel's experience that you should take to heart.

1. Briefly outline 8:1-20 and 10:12-22.

    8:1-20 _____

    _____

    _____

    _____

    _____

    _____

For Thought and Discussion: a. When Satan tempted Jesus in the wilderness, the Son of Man resisted by quoting Deuteronomy 8:3, 6:13, and 6:16 to Himself (see Luke 4:4,8,12). All three verses came from the account of Israel's training in the wilderness. Why do you think Jesus quoted this part of Deuteronomy? What can we learn from His example?
   b. Why did God have Jesus experience what Israel experienced (see Deuteronomy 8:2-3; Luke 4:1-2; Hebrews 2:11,17-18; 5:8)?

10:12-22 _____

Is God able?
Is God necessary?

2. Observe how God provided for Israel in the wilderness (see 8:3-4,15-16). Why did God make His people spend forty years in the desert with just enough food, water, and necessities for survival?

8:2 _____

8:3 _____

8:5 _____

3. What do you think the people should have learned about the Lord from their experiences in the desert?

_____

_____

_____

_____

_____

**For Thought and
Discussion:** In
Deuteronomy 7:17-22
and 8:17-18, Moses
warned the Israelites
not to trust their own
strength or fear their
own weakness. What
can Christians learn
from meditating
on these passages?
(Compare John
15:4-5; 2 Corinthians
1:8-11; 4:7-12; 12:7-10;
Galatians 3:3.)

4. When the Israelites gain more than the bare
essentials in the Promised Land, how should
their desert experience continue to affect them?

8:10 _____

_____

_____

8:11 _____

_____

_____

_____

5. What sinful attitudes will prosperity tempt them
to adopt (see 8:12-14,17)?

_____

_____

_____

_____

_____

_____

6. Why is it important that *God* is the one who
gives the ability to produce wealth (see 8:18)?

_____

_____

_____

_____

Optional Application: Has God ever brought you into a "wilderness" to learn to depend on Him (see Deuteronomy 8:2-5)? If so, write down a description of the experience and what you learned from it. Who could you share this story with?

_____

_____

_____

7. How is 8:1-18 relevant to your life? List some lessons you would like to apply to your attitudes and priorities.

_____

_____

_____

_____

_____

_____

_____

Is God worthy?

8. Since God is going to provide everything His people need, how should they respond (see 10:12,16)?

_____

_____

_____

_____

_____

_____

_____

9. Why is God worthy of this response? List as many reasons as you can find.

10:14 _____

_____

_____

_____

_____

_____

10:15 _____

_____

_____

_____

10:17 _____

_____

_____

_____

10:21 _____

_____

_____

_____

_____

10:22 _____

_____

_____

_____

For Further Study:
Why does Moses repeat what he says in 10:12 so often?

Optional Application: a. How can you cultivate a healthy fear of God (Deuteronomy 10:12; Proverbs 1:7)? Using a concordance, study the word *fear* in the Bible.

b. How can you serve God with all your heart and soul? Meditate on 10:12 this week and look for ways to practice it.

Circumcise (10:16). A ritual cutting away of the foreskin, which signified that a man was a Jew. It was supposed to demonstrate that a man had committed himself to obeying the Lord; it symbolized blood sacrifice and the consequences of rebelling against the covenant—God would "cut off" the rebel and his heirs from Israel (see Genesis 17:9-14).[1]

For a New Testament view of circumcision, see Romans 2:28-29.

Optional
Application: The
Lord urges us to
love the fatherless,
widows, and aliens
(see 10:18-19). Do you
know any children
whose fathers are
absent, women
without husbands,
or strangers in your
area? What help do
they need, and how
can you give that aid?

10. What does it mean to circumcise your heart (see 10:16)?

_____

_____

_____

_____

_____

_____

Study Skill—Connecting Words

Connecting words are clues to the logic in a passage. Connectives may show:

Time: *after, as, before, then, until, when, while*;

Place: *where*;

Purpose: *in order that, so that*;

Contrast: *although, but, much more, nevertheless, otherwise, yet*;

Comparison: *also, as, as . . . so, just as . . . so, likewise, so also*;

Source: *by means of, from, through*

For example, the word *therefore* in 10:16 connects that verse to 10:14-15. Be alert for connecting words as you study.

11. Give two reasons why God's people should "love" strangers and anyone who is powerless (see 10:19).

10:17-18 _____

_____

_____

_____

10:19 _____

_____

_____

116

Does God really love me?

12. Moses says that obedience to the Lord's laws is for Israel's own good (see 10:13). How is obedience for our own good (see Deuteronomy 6:24; John 15:9-17; Romans 8:6)?

_____

_____

_____

_____

_____

_____

The Torah today

For Further Study: As preachers often do, Moses reiterates his main points (see chapter 11). Summarize each paragraph of this chapter in a sentence or title.

For Further Study: Summarize as best you can the basic requirements of the covenant between God and Israel. (What did God agree to do? What did Israel agree to do?) See 10:12-17 or 6:20-25.

For Thought and Discussion: According to Psalm 139:23-24, Romans 8:26-27, and Hebrews 4:12, how can we uproot hidden doubts about God?

Study Skill—Application

Hebrews 3:12 says that doubts about God grow from roots in a "sinful, unbelieving heart." The verse is addressed to Christians who do believe that Jesus is Lord and Savior but who may still have doubts buried deep in their hearts, their subconscious hidden places. Such doubts can arise from childhood experiences; for instance, feeling that a parent often failed us can make it difficult for us to trust God to meet our needs.[2] If we find ourselves acting as though we doubt God, we can look for roots of these doubts in our hearts. (See Luke 6:43-45, Romans 8:26-27, Hebrews 4:12.)

A caution: Don't begin digging around in your subconscious or memories for roots of all your current problems. Instead, let the Holy Spirit bring roots to light in His timing. We do not always need to know the causes of our besetting sins in order to abandon them. Also, churning up lots of unresolved feelings all at once can make you focus on self and paralyze your service to God and others.

**Optional
Application:** Moses
told the Israelites
to remember God's
deeds whenever
they were tempted
to doubt Him. On
what acts of God can
you meditate when
you find yourself
doubting Him? Name
some events in your
personal history and
in the church's history.

**Optional
Application:** Do you
have difficulty fully
trusting that God
is *willing* or *able* to
meet your needs?
Or do you often act
as though He isn't
necessary for your
survival or *worthy*
of your obedience?
If so, choose verses
from chapters 8–11
to meditate on, and
ask God to reveal the
roots of your unbelief.

13. Choose a verse or verses from this lesson (such
    as 8:3, 8:18, 10:12, or 10:18-19) and write down
    the truth in that verse that you would like to
    apply to your life.

    _____

    _____

    _____

    _____

    _____

    _____

14. Take some time to think and pray about this
    truth. Is there anything specific you can do to
    act on it during the coming week? If so, note
    your plans here.

    _____

    _____

    _____

    _____

    _____

15. (*Optional*) Summarize the main things you
    learned from this lesson.

    _____

    _____

    _____

    _____

    _____

    _____

16. If you have any questions about chapters 8 or 10, record them here.

_____

_____

_____

_____

_____

_____

Transition

Deuteronomy 11:26-32 prepares for the next three sections of the book by stating their topics in reverse order. Deuteronomy 11:26-28 summarizes the blessings and curses pronounced fully in 28:1-68. Deuteronomy 11:29-30 mentions the covenant renewal ceremony on Mounts Gerizim and Ebal described in 27:1-26. Deuteronomy 11:31-32 repeats the exhortation to obey the commands to be heard "today"—the "decrees" and "laws" of 12:1–26:19.

For the group

Most Christians know that God doesn't deserve to be doubted. But willpower can only bury a doubt, not erase it, and feeling guilty about doubt doesn't help us trust God. The Lord knew how often subtle doubts would trouble Israel, so He gave Moses words of encouragement for the people.

Many people find it hard to admit that they sometimes doubt that God knows what He is doing in their lives. At some point in your discussion, such as during application, you might want to help group members accept their own and each other's doubts. It is sin to doubt God, but it is the sort of sin that almost every sinful human commits frequently. The apostle John writes that it is a much more serious sin to tell ourselves and others that we do not sin in this way (see 1 John 1:8-10).

Warm-up. Ask a few people to share one time when they were tempted to doubt God—His power, love, justice, worthiness, or whatever.

Observation/Interpretation. Moses overcomes Israel's doubts by recounting stories from the people's history and facts they know about God. You can structure your discussion like this:
1. Have someone name a doubt about God.
2. Ask someone to give an example of how a Christian might experience a similar doubt.
3. Let someone briefly retell the story or facts Moses recounted to overcome the doubt. (For instance, the Exodus should dispel the fear that God is not able to help Israel [see 7:17-19]. The desert experience should prove that He is willing, able, and necessary. The facts in 10:14-22 should prove Him worthy of allegiance.)
4. How do these reminders help you to overcome your own doubts? How should you act in light of what Moses says?

Application. Give everyone a chance to share how this lesson applies to a situation he or she is currently facing. Is anyone struggling with a reluctance to trust or obey God in any areas? As a group, plan a strategy for dealing with this kind of temptation. If you like, look at Luke 4:1-13 for Jesus' example.

Prayer. Encourage members to confess any doubts if they feel comfortable doing so. Members should know that nothing shared in the group will be revealed outside and also that no one will be pressured to share. Ask God to confirm His trustworthy character to each of you. Praise Him for being necessary, able, and willing to meet your needs. Thank Him for what He has done in your own lives to demonstrate His trustworthiness. Ask Him to uproot the hidden doubts in your hearts.

Plan to pray for each other during the coming week with regard to the struggles you shared.

Optional lessons. Pages 123–126 introduce the laws in 12:1–26:19. Each group member should read that material whether or not you plan to do any of the optional lessons at this point. If you do plan to do any of them, encourage each person to get a notebook or some paper for answers, discussion notes, and applications. If you want a break from intense lesson preparation, just ask everyone to read the passages you plan to discuss and the background material, without writing any answers. You can answer the questions when you meet as a group.

Either now or after lesson 12 is a good time to do an optional lesson or two. You might let the group choose a topic that interests most people.

The Lowly

"There will always be poor people in the land." God promised (see Deuteronomy 15:11). Deuteronomy names only several types of people in Israel who were vulnerable to their more secure neighbors.

The *resident alien* (see 10:18) had an official legal status. He had fewer rights than a citizen, who had to belong to the dominant local tribe, and more rights than a traveling foreigner. Any foreigner could expect hospitality when he visited, but he was not entitled to join in religious rites, take field gleanings or tithes, and so on. By contrast, a resident alien could not be made to work on the Sabbath (see Deuteronomy 5:14), could gather leavings from the harvest (see 24:19-21), was included in the Lord's feasts (see 16:11,14), deserved love and equal justice in a dispute with an Israelite (see 1:16; 10:19; 24:17), shared in the tithe in the third year (see 14:28-29), and had to obey Israelite laws against pagan worship and magic (see Leviticus 17:8-16). Aliens could own no land and so could only become hired laborers (see page 195), merchants, craftsmen, or herdsmen. In Israel, all conquered Canaanites were aliens, as were any immigrants.

The *fatherless* and *widows* were extremely vulnerable because families rather than the state had first responsibility for people. But widows and orphans lacked wage-earning and land-owning family. Since there were few wage-earning jobs for a woman with children, the whole tribe was expected to be family for those who lacked their own. The Lord promised to be Father to those who had no father.[3]

121

1. Kenneth Barker, ed., *The NIV Study Bible* (Grand Rapids, MI: Zondervan, 1985), 31.
2. John and Paula Sandford, *The Transformation of the Inner Man* (Plainfield, NJ: Bridge Publishing, 1982), 23–38.
3. Roland de Vaux, *Ancient Israel,* vol. 1 (New York: McGraw-Hill, 1965), 39–40, 74–76.

DEUTERONOMY 12:1–26:19

Introduction to the Laws

In chapters 12–26, Moses preaches on some of the detailed stipulations of the covenant. He defines how the nation will "fear . . . walk . . . love . . . serve . . . and observe" (10:12-13) in the Promised Land.

Why the laws?

Deuteronomy 12:1–26:19 closely parallels the so-called Book of the Covenant, Exodus 20:22-23:19. The laws in Exodus were given at the beginning of the wilderness trek. In about half the laws in Deuteronomy, Moses expounded upon laws in Exodus, interpreting them for new situations and urging reasons for obedience. In a way, these chapters of Deuteronomy are like a sermon on Exodus—the last sermon Moses ever gave. Comparing Exodus and Deuteronomy reveals some of what the Lord taught Moses during the desert wandering about how the people could live together justly.

When God gave the laws in Deuteronomy, Israel was a league of tribes bound together only by their allegiance to the Lord. For four hundred years, they had lived in settled villages in Egypt, raising crops and animals. After one generation of desert wandering, they were going to return to this settled life in Canaan. However, Israel's ancestors had been nomadic (wandering) shepherds. Although the Israelites had lost many of their nomadic ancestors' customs, they retained some crucial ones.

For example, an Israelite's first loyalty was to his family. He related to God as a member of a group, not as an individual. He defended the interests of his family or tribe when they conflicted with those of the nation; it was hard for the Israelites to see themselves as one nation under the Lord. According to ancient custom, people took personal vengeance on behalf of family, clan, or tribe, sometimes killing a whole family or destroying much property in revenge for one person's insult or injury. People normally judged actions rather than motives. Strength prevailed; war was unrestricted; tradition was hard to break.

These beliefs can help us understand some of the laws in Deuteronomy.

123

The commands are meant for a tribal society changing from nomadic to settled life. Through the laws, the Lord was going to train a people to enter more and more deeply into relationship with Him (see Galatians 3:24). Fourteen hundred years of wrestling with this Law was going to prepare Israel for the Savior.

The Law had to help Israel not only grow out of past customs but also resist conforming to the present practices of pagan neighbors. The Canaanites, who occupied the land Israel was entering, were an organized agricultural society. They were more sophisticated than Israel, but their ethics resembled Israel's tribal ones (personal vengeance, few legal procedures, and so on). The Canaanites tried to use magic to manipulate the many spirits and forces of nature (see "Canaanite Religion" on pages 100 and 169), and their idea of holiness was power without morality (see page 95).

Thus, to prepare His people for Christ, the Lord needed to transform (1) the people from a band of tribes into a nation, (2) their notion of divinity from many gods to the One True God, (3) their understanding of holiness, (4) their personal ethics, and (5) their concept of justice. To accomplish this transformation, He had to call the people to reject both their own ancient traditions and the example of their new neighbors in Canaan. The Law of Moses was designed to accomplish this task of preparing Israel for Christ.

Christians and the Law

Most Christians have one of three attitudes toward the laws in Deuteronomy 12:1–26:19:

1. These laws were meant only for the nation of Israel and have no relevance for Christians.

2. The laws are applications of the Ten Commandments to Israelite society. We can learn from them about God's character and His principles of justice. Those principles can be adapted and applied to our own civil life. Applying these principles of justice is not necessary for salvation, but it is part of our sanctification (the process of acquiring a holy character and learning to live a holy life).

3. Except for the laws of ritual and sacrifice (fulfilled in Christ), Christians should keep all of the Old Testament laws (see Matthew 5:17-18). They are not necessary for salvation, but they describe in detail how God desires His people to live. Christians in democratic states should try to influence their governments to make the civil laws conform as much as possible to the Old Testament standard.[1]

If we accept view (1), there is no point in studying Deuteronomy 12–26. However, if we take view (2) or (3), there is a point. Even if we decide that the specific laws are not binding upon us as the Ten Commandments are, the laws can still teach us about God's love, justice, and mercy and about man's need for atonement for falling short of God's expectations. The commands to love God and neighbor still apply to us, and the laws in Deuteronomy show how God taught Israel to love God and neighbor.

However, because you may not be interested in all the topics the laws address, we have put seven optional lessons on 12:1–26:19 in the back of this study guide (pages 163–214). If you prefer not to take time for seven lessons, you might want to put together one or two lessons from the optional material. You can study a lesson in its entirety or select sections from different lessons for one study. You can do the optional lessons now or wait until after lesson 12. You may want to get a notebook to jot down answers and applications.

If you decide not to use any of the optional lessons, you should at least skim through chapters 12–26 to see what's there. If you find topics that interest you, you can find the questions on those passages in the optional section. Or you can come back to this part of Deuteronomy later on.

What the laws cover

Here are some of the topics God covers in 12:1–26:19 (the capital letters and titles correspond to the optional lessons):

Loving God

A. "Pure Worship" deals with how the Lord tried to keep His people from adopting the attitudes and practices of the culture around them. In chapter 12, Moses gives commands about avoiding pagan worship and teaches the distinctions between Creator and created, holy and common.
B. "Prophecy and Magic" continues the same theme: Why Israel should look to the Lord for knowledge and power. The study explores reasons for the laws on (1) true prophets, (2) forbidden knowledge, (3) dealing with false prophets, and (4) magic.
C. "Ceremonies of Holiness" covers the reasons for and meanings of (1) the dietary laws, and (2) Israel's three major feasts: Passover, Pentecost, and Tabernacles.

Loving Neighbor

D. "Tithes and Loans" clarifies the laws on these two subjects and examines them for principles of giving that Christians might apply.
E. "More Economics" covers laws on (1) wages, (2) gleaning, (3) hospitality, (4) the year of release from debts, and (5) slavery. God's vision for economic justice in Israel is the issue here.
F. "Justice in the Courts" deals with (1) choosing judges, (2) fair trials, (3) the king, (4) fair punishment, and (5) murder.
G. "War, Women, Kindness, Crime" covers (1) the holy war, (2) people who were barred from legally becoming members of Israel, (3) women, (4) laws on neighborliness, and (5) the crimes of the rebellious son and the kidnapper.

A Christian might find many of these laws of interest. For instance, parts of the laws on murder foreshadow Christ and are quoted in the New Testament. The section on women includes the divorce law Jesus explains in

Matthew 5:31-32. The rules on membership in Israel shed light on the new covenant. The laws on worship illustrate holiness, purity, and trust. The economic and judicial laws reflect timeless principles of justice.

One way of sampling the laws might be to select parts of the first three lessons for one study on loving God, and parts of the last four for one study on loving your neighbor. Or you could make one study that samples both aspects of the law. Third, you could ask each group member to choose one section that interests him, study it, and briefly share with the group what he learned from it about God, Christ, justice, and so on.

As you study each law, ask yourself why God might have given it, what principles lie behind it, and how the same principles, if not the same law, might apply today. Consider how each law expands on one or more of the Ten Commandments.

1. For more information on these three views of the laws, see Peter Craigie's *The Book of Deuteronomy*, Gordon Fee and Douglas Stuart's *How to Read the Bible for All Its Worth*, or James B. Jordan's *The Law of the Covenant*.

DEUTERONOMY 27:1–28:68

Covenant Renewal

*"Be silent, O Israel, and listen. You have now
become the people of the LORD your God."*
Deuteronomy 27:9

Moses was going to die, and the generation who
heard him in Moab would not live forever either.
Generations would grow up who had experienced
none of the desert wandering. So God commanded
that every seven years, the people would gather
to renew their promises of loyalty to Him, their
Sovereign Lord.[1] In that way, each generation would
be reminded repeatedly that loyalty to God was the
life-and-death issue they faced.

Deuteronomy 27:1–31:29 followed many of the
closing features of ancient Near Eastern treaties.
Some treaties invoked gods to bless loyal subjects
and curse treaty-breakers, just as Moses promised
that the Lord would bless or curse (see 27:1–28:68).
Some treaties required periodic renewal in ceremonies like the ones described in 27:1-26 and 31:9-13.
Some recapitulated their basic elements, as Moses
did in his third speech, 29:1–30:20.

In this lesson, you will look at the blessings and
curses of the renewal ceremony that Israel was supposed to hold every seven years. Try to envision the
event Moses is commanding. From 11:26-30, recall
that the ceremony took place at Mounts Gerizim
and Ebal (see the map on page 31) near Shechem.
There was a road through a valley from Shechem
to Samaria; Mount Gerizim lay to the south of the
road, and Mount Ebal to the north. As one looked
east toward the Jordan, Gerizim was on the right,
the side of favor and blessing (see Genesis 35:18;

127

For Further Study:
According to 27:9-10, did the Lord choose people because they obeyed Him, or did they obey because He had chosen them?

Matthew 25:33-34). Ebal was on the left, the side of cursing (see Matthew 25:33,41). Representatives from six tribes would invoke the curses upon themselves for disobedience while standing on Mount Ebal, and the representatives from the other six would invoke blessings for obedience while standing on Mount Gerizim (see Deuteronomy 11:29; 27:11-26). When Israel swore this oath of allegiance, the two mountains would become the "two witnesses" required to convict a person of sin (see 17:6; 19:15).[2]

When Joshua held the covenant renewal ceremony seven years later, he did just what Deuteronomy 27:1-26 commanded. Then he read from Moses' speeches in Deuteronomy and added some exhortation of his own (see Joshua 8:30-35).

Read 27:1–28:68 at least once before beginning the questions in this lesson. Don't get bogged down in the details of the blessings and curses.

When (27:2,4). (Literally, "on the day" in 27:2). This did not necessarily mean "as soon as." It would have taken the Israelites some time to penetrate to Mount Ebal (some twenty miles from the Jordan).

Plaster (27:2,4). This would make the writing stand out clearly.

Burnt offerings . . . fellowship offerings (27:6-7). See the box "Sacrifice: Old Testament Grace" on page 90.

1. Israel was supposed to set up two things on Mount Ebal. Each object represented something important to the Israelite faith. What did each represent? What function did each serve?

   the plastered stones inscribed with the covenant

   _____
   _____
   _____
   _____

_____
_____
_____
the altar for sacrifices _____
_____
_____
_____
_____
_____

For Thought and Discussion: Christians don't hold covenant renewal ceremonies like the ones Israel held, but do we do anything that serves the same purpose? If so, what? If not, why not?

2. a. What was supposed to happen at the covenant renewal ceremony (see 27:12-26)?

_____
_____
_____
_____

   b. What was the meaning or purpose of these events?

_____
_____
_____
_____

3. a. After the responsive oaths, Moses described the blessings and curses that the people were calling down on themselves. What blessings could an obedient people expect (see 28:1-14)?

_____

For Thought and
Discussion: Moses
elaborated the curses
graphically and at
length. Why do you
think he did this?

_____

_____

_____

_____

_____

b. Briefly summarize the misfortunes that
   would befall Israel if the people disobeyed (see
   28:15-68).

_____

_____

_____

_____

_____

_____

The Torah today

4. The law posted on Ebal, the altar of sacrifice,
   and the blessings and curses all proclaim truths
   about God and man that are basic to the New
   Testament.

   a. Why was the covenant treaty on the
      mountain of cursing (see Romans 3:19-20;
      4:15; 7:7-8; Deuteronomy 31:26-27)?

   _____

   _____

   _____

   _____

   _____

_____

_____

b. Why was an altar for sacrifice also necessary
on the mountain of cursing (see Leviticus
4:13-14; Hebrews 9:22)?

_____

_____

_____

_____

c. What New Testament principles do the
blessings and curses declare (see Romans 2:6-
13; 6:23; Galatians 6:7-8)?

_____

_____

_____

_____

_____

_____

5. How does God's Word fulfill for us the same
function that the covenant posted on Mount
Ebal fulfilled (see Romans 3:20; Hebrews
4:12-13)?

_____

_____

_____

_____

_____

For Thought and Discussion: In your experience, does God generally bless your obedience and allow bad consequences of your disobedience? Can you explain your experience from biblical (especially New Testament) teaching?

For Thought and Discussion: Why does a Christian want not to sin even though he is free from the Law's curses (see Romans 6:1-23)?

6. How does Jesus do for us what the sacrifices did for Israel (see Romans 3:21-26; Hebrews 9:11-14; 10:1-14)?

_____

_____

_____

_____

_____

_____

7. The Israelites invited God to curse them if they broke His commands (see Deuteronomy 27:12-26). Why do Christians not do this (see Galatians 3:10-14)?

_____

_____

_____

_____

_____

8. Because of Jesus, Israel's covenant renewal ceremony no longer applies to us. However, have you learned from 27:1–28:68 any principles or attitudes that are relevant to the Christian life? If so, what are they?

_____

_____

_____

_____

_____

9. Is there anything in this lesson that you would
   like to meditate or act on? If so, what are your
   plans?

   _____

   _____

   _____

   _____

   _____

   _____

   _____

   _____

10. List any questions you have about 27:1–28:68.

   _____

   _____

   _____

For the group

Warm-up. Ask the group why they are studying
the Old Testament Law. One purpose is probably to
understand the New Testament gospel better. This
will lead smoothly into the focus of this lesson: how
the covenant renewal ceremony foreshadows and
explains the new covenant under Christ.

Discussion. Structure your discussion by examining two facets of each aspect of the ceremony:

   1. What did each aspect (the inscribed stones,
the altar, the invocation of curses, and so on) mean
for Israel? What did God want Israel to learn from
this aspect?

   2. How is each aspect fulfilled by Christ, or how
does it explain or correspond to something in the
Christian faith?

   For example, the monument inscribed with
the covenant was the Word of God, the Law that

133

witnessed against Israel, testifying to the nation's sin. Likewise, God's Word convicts modern people of sin, leading us to repent and seek atonement and forgiveness.

Once you've grasped how these chapters illuminate the New Testament, discuss how you can apply what you've learned. Does God's Word witness against you, urging you to repent in some area? Are you moved to thank God (and live in gratitude) for delivering you from the curse of the Law? Perhaps you can take time as a group to give thanks for this deliverance.

Worship.

1. When we say that the covenant was "renewed" every seven years, we don't mean that God gave new, slightly different commands at each ceremony. Rather, the leaders reminded the people of what God had said, and the people renewed their commitment to the commands.
2. J. A. Thompson, *Deuteronomy: An Introduction and Commentary* (London: InterVarsity, 1974), 157.

DEUTERONOMY 29:1–30:20

Choose Life

"This day I call heaven and earth as witnesses against you that I have set before you life and death, blessings and curses. Now choose life, so that you and your children may live and that you may love the LORD your God. . . . For the LORD is your life."

Deuteronomy 30:19-20

For how many days had the Israelites been standing in the hot sun on the plains of Moab, listening to their leader preach the sermons that became the book of Deuteronomy (see 29:10-15)? He was indeed repeating himself in his passion to melt their stubborn hearts. But ancient covenants normally ended with a recapitulation of their basic terms, so Moses did the same thing in his third speech (see 29:1–30:20). In this speech, Moses reached the climax of his sermon—the exhortation to "choose life." Read 29:1–30:20.

1. Write a title for each section of 29:1–30:20.

   29:1 _____

   _____

   29:2-8 _____

   _____

   29:9-15 _____

   _____

135

For Thought and Discussion: Exactly what does Israel not understand (see 29:4)?

Optional Application: Think about what might have kept Israel from receiving a heart that understands (see 29:4). Specifically, how can you make yourself more open to this gift?

29:16-29 _____

_____

30:1-10 _____

_____

30:11-14 _____

_____

· 30:15-20 _____

_____

Circumcised hearts (29:1–30:14)

A mind that understands (29:4). Literally, "a heart that understands." The problem is not purely intellectual, as 30:11-14 makes clear.

2. As before, Moses began by reminding Israel of the acts of kindness that proved the Lord deserved allegiance (see 29:2-8). God's acts of grace included the miraculous deliverance from slavery, provision for every need in the wilderness, the gift of the Promised Land, and above all, the gifts of relationship with God and righteous laws to live by.

   God blessed Israel with His Word, but what grace did He withhold from His people (29:4)?

_____

_____

_____

_____

_____

3. What did God already know was going to happen because He had withheld this gift (see 29:16-28)? Summarize briefly.

_____

136

_____

_____

_____

_____

_____

4. What attitude did Moses call a "root . . . that
   produces . . . bitter poison" (29:18-19)?

_____

_____

_____

_____

_____

_____

5. The writer to the Hebrews gives the same
   warning to Christians (see Hebrews 12:15). How
   might a Christian have bitter roots in him that
   produce the poison of Deuteronomy 29:18-19?

_____

_____

_____

_____

_____

_____

The LORD _uprooted them_ (29:28). What Moses
   predicted in 29:16-28 came to pass so accurately that liberal scholars have even suggested
   that the chapter must have been written after
   the events took place. Israel fell into material-
   ism and idolatry, the nation split in two, and
   the northern half was conquered by Assyria.

For Further Study:
Using a concordance
and a fairly literal
translation such as
KJV or NASB, list
everything Moses
says in Deuteronomy
about the people's
hearts.

The Assyrians deported the Israelites to other parts of the Near East and repopulated Israel with pagans. A century later, the unrepentant southern nation (called Judah) was crushed by the Babylonians, and its people were exiled (see 1–2 Kings). After seventy years, God allowed some of the exiles who had rededicated themselves to the Lord to return to Judah (see Ezra and Nehemiah). However, those returned Jews began to stray from the Lord again almost immediately, and the Romans destroyed the Jewish nation forty years after Jesus Christ was crucified. From then until this century, there have been almost no Jews in the Promised Land.

6. When the results of Israel's sin were fulfilled and Israel was dispersed among the nations, what did God say His people would do (see 30:1-2)?

_____

_____

_____

_____

_____

_____

7. How would God respond to Israel's desire to repent (see 30:3-7)?

_____

_____

_____

_____

_____

_____

8. The Israelites failed to obey God because they lacked hearts that could understand God (see 29:4), but God promised that eventually He would "circumcise" their hearts (see 30:6). Recall the meaning of circumcised hearts from question 10 of lesson 9 (see page 116). How do the following passages explain what God was going to do to His people's hearts?

Jeremiah 31:31-34 _____

_____

_____

_____

_____

Ezekiel 36:24-28 _____

_____

_____

_____

_____

9. The Israelites did not yet have circumcised hearts, however (see Deuteronomy 10:16, 29:4), so they were likely to make excuses when they failed to obey God. What excuses does Moses warn against in 30:11-14?

_____

_____

_____

_____

_____

Not too difficult (30:11). KJV renders "not hidden."

For Thought and Discussion: In light of 29:4, what does Moses mean by saying in 30:11-14 that the Law is "not too difficult for you or beyond your reach"?

Optional Application: Do you ever make excuses for not living by God's Word like the ones in 30:11-14? If so, why are these excuses especially unacceptable now that Christ and the Spirit are available to us (see Romans 8:5-13; 10:5-11)?

For Further Study: In Romans 10:5-11, Paul applies to the Word of Christ what Moses says about God's Old Testament Word in Deuteronomy 30:11-14. What does Paul's commentary reveal about the relationship between Christ and the Law?

10. What was the real reason Israel failed to obey God (see 29:4,18-19)?

_____

_____

_____

_____

_____

11. Based on what you have studied in Deuteronomy, why is it essential that Christ has circumcised our hearts and put His Holy Spirit in us (see John 14:26; Romans 8:13; Colossians 2:11-12)?

_____

_____

_____

_____

_____

Choice (30:15-20)

12. In 30:15-20, Moses states the stark choice facing Israel. What are the alternatives (see 30:15,19)?

_____

_____

_____

or _____

_____

13. Do modern people face the same choices that you wrote in question 12? If so, how can a person choose life, blessing, and prosperity

140

today (see Romans 10:9-11; Acts 2:37-39; Luke 9:23-24)?

_____

_____

_____

_____

_____

_____

For Further Study: If a person chooses life with Jesus, what blessings can he expect? (See, for example, Luke 6:20-23; 9:23-25; 12:22-32; 18:29-30; John 15:14-16; Romans 5:1-5)

14. As a Christian, can you also say that "the LORD is your life" (Deuteronomy 30:20)? If so, what does this mean for you?

_____

_____

_____

_____

_____

_____

15. What do you learn about God from the choice He gave Israel?

_____

_____

_____

_____

_____

The Torah today

16. In one or two sentences, summarize the most important insights you have had from 29:1–30:20.

_____

141

Optional Application: Many people are uninterested in Jesus because He does not seem to be a life-or-death issue (see 30:19). Think of someone you know who is not interested. What does matter to him or her? How can you lead him to see that the Bible speaks to what are life-and-death issues to him?

Optional Application: What is one practical way in which you could "choose life" in your thoughts, priorities, and actions this week?

Optional Application: Choose some verses from this passage to meditate on for the next week, such as 29:4, 29:12-15, 29:18, 30:1-8, 30:11-14, 30:15, or 30:19-20.

17. How might you respond in prayer or action to what you have studied in this lesson? Is there some verse you might meditate on, someone you might speak to, or some action you might take?

_____

_____

_____

_____

_____

_____

18. List any questions you have about anything in this lesson.

_____

_____

_____

_____

_____

For the group

Set the scene for the group: The whole nation is still standing before Moses, committing themselves and their descendants to the terms of God's covenant (see 29:10-15). Joshua will do the same seven years later (see Joshua 8:30-35), and successive leaders will repeat the ceremony.

Draw attention to Moses' emotion in these chapters. He is passionately imploring the people to see the life-or-death issues facing them. Will they rebel or remain faithful? Moses already knows both the decision they will make mentally now and the real heart-choice their actions will ultimately reveal. Yet, although the outcome is known, the choice is still real.

Warm-up. Let each person think of one issue in his or her life that currently seems like a life-or-death matter, something on which life and prosperity seem to depend.

Questions. The lesson focuses on the similarities and differences between the situation facing Israel and the one facing people today. You will essentially be comparing the new and old covenants. In a veiled manner, Moses summarizes most of the history of salvation: God chose a people and gave them the old covenant; they failed to keep it, so God made a new covenant and worked some mighty deeds in order that His people could keep His covenant.

To contrast Israel and us, discuss: What exactly was the heart-circumcision or heart-understanding that Israel lacked? What difference does it make to us that we have this circumcision? How does a person obtain it?

Draw attention to the fact that God knew when He gave His covenant that Israel would not obey it. Why is this important? Was God cruel to give a Law without giving the grace to keep it? Does 29:4 relieve Israel of responsibility for being unable to keep the covenant? How does this withholding of grace fit into God's plan of salvation?

Don't forget application. Israel was guilty for not choosing life and reaped the consequences, even though the people lacked circumcised hearts. Since God has given us circumcised hearts, how should we respond to 29:1–30:20? A caution: Our possession of God's power does not make us less dependent on God's daily grace than Israel was; if anything, we are more dependent. Discuss practical ways to "choose life" and obey God in light of the utterly dependent attitude of John 15:1-5, 2 Corinthians 12:9-10, and Galatians 2:20.

Prayer. Thank God for giving you circumcised hearts. Ask Him for the daily grace to choose life this week.

The Secret Things and the Things Revealed

Deuteronomy 29:29 is difficult. Moses explained in 18:9-14 how God viewed people who attempted to learn "the secret things"—matters that God hid from men for their own ultimate good. As for "the things revealed," the Torah was God's fullest revelation of Himself up to that point, yet it fell far short of the revelation He would make in Jesus. In 29:29, God was probably saying that the Israelites should seek to live up to the revelation they have as well as possible and let God worry about what He had not told them.

God had His reasons for not sending Jesus yet. Do you think He held Israelites accountable for not believing in Jesus? What do you think He held them accountable for (see Romans 2:12-15)?

In John 21:21-22, Jesus advises Peter not to worry about John's future but to obey Jesus without having all his curiosity satisfied. Deuteronomy 29:29 may be good counsel for us, who wonder about people in other times and places who have had no opportunity to hear the gospel, and who want all the answers before we begin to follow Jesus. Do you think someone in your society who dismisses Jesus without investigating His claims has the same excuse that an Israelite had? What does Deuteronomy 29:29 have to say about this?

144

DEUTERONOMY 31:1–34:12

Moses' Farewell

"See now that I myself am He! There is no god besides me. I put to death and I bring to life, I have wounded and I will heal, and no one can deliver out of my hand."

Deuteronomy 32:39

Moses was a man of many gifts. Just before his death at 120 years of age, he wrote for Israel a beautiful song in praise of God. Then he pronounced a series of blessings which prophesied Israel's future. And, finally, he climbed Mount Nebo, passed his office to Joshua, and gave himself to the Lord. These final words and actions offer us insight into this man, but more important, they give us insight into his God.

Read 31:1–34:12, asking God to reveal Himself to you.

Optional Application: Do you need to "be strong and courageous" to do something God wants? If so, meditate on 31:6.

Two witnesses (31:1–32:47)

1. As he handed leadership over to Joshua, Moses exhorted both the people and Joshua to "be strong and courageous" (31:6,7,23) and not to fear (see 31:6,8).

   Why was this instruction so important that it needed to be repeated?

   _____

   _____

   _____

For Thought and Discussion: What do Christians read repeatedly, as the Israelites reread the Law? Why do we do this?

For Thought and Discussion: Why do you suppose the Lord made a covenant with Israel, knowing beforehand that they would break it?

_____

_____

Gave it to the priests (31:9). "Ancient treaties specified that a copy of the treaty was to be placed before the gods at the religious centers of the nations involved. For Israel, that meant to place it in the ark of the covenant"[1] (33:9).

Also, one of the priests' main duties was to read and teach the Law to Israel, both at the covenant renewal ceremony and at times between ceremonies (see Deuteronomy 31:10-13; 33:10; Malachi 2:4-9).

2. Every seven years at the Feast of Tabernacles, the Levites were supposed to read the book of Deuteronomy to the people (see 31:10-12). What was the purpose of this provision (see 31:12-13)?

_____

_____

_____

_____

_____

3. Explain one reason why Moses wrote the song of chapter 32 (see 31:15-22,28-30).

_____

_____

_____

_____

_____

_____

Heaven and earth (32:1). In the ancient Near East, a sovereign with a rebel vassal would summon him to undergo legal proceedings. The evidence of two witnesses was sufficient to convict the rebel (see 19:15). Also, "the typical ancient covenant outside the Old Testament contained a list of gods who served as "witnesses" to its provisions."[2] Instead of pagan gods, the Lord called heaven and earth as His witnesses. The Law stored in the ark and posted on Mount Ebal testified to the agreement between God and Israel; heaven and earth would testify that Israel had accepted the terms and then broken them.

For Thought and Discussion: Choose some of the words you wrote in question 6 and explain why the Lord is described like this.

4. What is another purpose of the song, according to 32:3?

_____

_____

_____

_____

5. Briefly summarize what the song is about (see 32:1-43).

_____

_____

_____

_____

_____

6. Read through the song (see 32:1-43) and record here the nouns, verbs, and phrases Moses uses to describe the Lord.

_____

_____

_____

_____

_____

_____

For Further Study:
Do a word study on *rock*, using a concordance. You might also trace the word *stone*.

___
___
___

Study Skill—Metaphors
A metaphor sheds new light on something by referring to it as something else—"All the world's a stage"—in order to imply a comparison between the two (usually dissimilar) things. The reference is not intended to be taken literally. The Lord is not a literal rock, of course; Moses is simply trying to tell us something about Him in using this image.

---

7. What might Moses have meant to convey by calling the Lord "the Rock" in 32:4,15,18,30-31?

___
___
___
___
___
___
___

Gave you birth (32:18). This phrase translates the Hebrew word for a mother giving birth. The Old Testament seldom used mother-imagery to describe the Lord (but see Isaiah 66:12-13). Its writers were constantly combating the worship of fertility goddesses such as Asherah. Despite confusion with the god Baal, the Lord generally preferred Israel to think of Him as Father rather than Mother.

8. What does the description of the Lord's double parenthood (see 32:18) tell you about Him?

148

_____

_____

_____

_____

_____

For Thought and Discussion:
a. Why does Israel ("Jeshurun") abandon God (see 32:15)?

b. Is there a warning here for Christians? If so, what is it?

For Thought and Discussion: Why was the pride of Israel's persecutors in 32:27 foolish (see 32:30,36,40-43)?

Enemy . . . adversary (32:27). Possibly Satan, or possibly Israel's earthly foes.

---

9. a. What would hold the Lord back from allowing Israel to suffer the final consequences of rebellion (see 32:26-27)?

_____

_____

_____

_____

b. What does this tell you about His character?

_____

_____

_____

_____

Final blessing (32:48–34:12)

Find Mount Nebo (see 32:49) on the map on page 31.
     Much of the blessing in chapter 33 envisions the historical situation of the eleventh century BC,[3] some two hundred years after Moses' death. *Reuben* (see 33:6) was repeatedly invaded and eventually overcome by Ammonites. *Simeon*, whom Moses did not mention, was absorbed into Judah in the eleventh century. *Judah* (see 33:7) was beset by

149

For Thought and Discussion: If you are familiar with the later history of Israel, think about why God revealed to Moses Israel's condition just before the nation took Saul as its first king. (Consider Deuteronomy 33:5; 1 Samuel 8:4-9.) If you do not know that history, read 1 and 2 Samuel and 1 and 2 Kings with this question in mind.

Optional Application: Think of one person with whom you could share the most significant truth you found in this lesson. Plan how you can communicate what seems important.

enemies in the eleventh century; Moses did not mention Judah's future as the royal tribe. *Ephraim* and *Manasseh*, the two half-tribes of Joseph (see 33:13-17), became the largest tribes of the northern part of the confederacy and came to dominate the north. *Dan* (see 33:22) was originally given territory in the south but moved north to Bashan in the twelfth or eleventh century.

10. Many of the good things Moses invoked upon the tribes in chapter 33 came to pass for a time. But they later failed when first the north and then the south of Israel was destroyed by enemies. From what you have read in Deuteronomy, why did the Israelites cease to experience these blessings?

   _____

   _____

   _____

   _____

   _____

11. What do you learn about the Lord from the ways Moses describes Him in the blessings (see 33:1-29)? (For instance, 33:2 says the Lord "dawned" and "shone.")

   _____

   _____

   _____

   _____

   _____

   _____

   _____

   _____

150

Servant of the LORD (34:5). A high official in the royal administration of the Great King. The title was given especially to Abraham (see Genesis 26:24), Moses (see Exodus 14:31), Joshua (see 24:29), David (see 2 Samuel 7:5), the prophets (see 2 Kings 9:7), Israel collectively (see Isaiah 41:8), and even a foreign king whom the Lord used (see Jeremiah 25:9).[4]

Face to face (34:10). Numbers 12:6-8 explains what this means.

12. Read the last events of Moses' life (see 34:1-8). In your own words, explain what was unique about Moses in Israel (see 34:9-12).

_____

_____

_____

_____

_____

The Torah today

13. a. Choose one of the images with which Moses described God in chapters 32–33 (questions 6–8,11). What does this image imply about how God will deal with you if you let Him?

_____

_____

_____

_____

_____

_____

_____

For Thought and Discussion: Who in the New Testament is the servant and prophet "like Moses, whom the Lord knew face to face" (34:10)?

For Further Study: How did Joshua obtain "the spirit of wisdom" (34:9)? Compare the situation in the new covenant that Peter describes in Acts 2:14-39.

151

Optional Application: Does the danger of prosperity (see 32:15-18; 8:17-18; 31:20) apply to you in any way? If so, how? Also, what truths about God and life can you meditate on to protect yourself from being deceived by prosperity? (For example, see Matthew 6:19-21; Philippians 1:21; 3:7-11, 18-21; James 5:1-6.)

Optional Application: Some verses you might meditate on this week are 31:6,8,20; 32:3-4,5,6,15,18,19-20,36,39.

b. How can you take this insight to heart and act on it this week?

_____

_____

_____

_____

_____

_____

_____

14. Is there anything else in 31:1–34:12 that you would like to remember and apply? (Consider the "Optional Applications" in this lesson.) If so, write down what you want to remember or do.

_____

_____

_____

_____

_____

15. List any questions you have about this lesson.

_____

_____

_____

_____

_____

_____

_____

For the group

In this lesson, look for insights into God's nature and how we should respond to it.

Warm-up. Ask members to name one thing that makes them anxious—a current or potential circumstance for instance. Afterward, move to question 1.

Two Witnesses.

1. Get brief answers to questions 2–4, as background to the song in chapter 32. You can use the second "Optional Application" on page 150 as a way to consider God's character.

2. Ask someone to summarize the song (question 5).

3. Together, compile a list of all the words and images Moses uses to describe God in his song: Rock, makes perfect works, faithful . . . avenger, atoner (question 6).

4. Delve into two or three of the images to see what they imply to you about God (questions 7 and 8).

5. Cover question 9 fairly briefly.

Blessings. Cover questions 10 and 12 quickly, but focus on question 11. You might simply add to the list of descriptions of God that you compiled from the song.

Application. Question 13 and the "Optional Application" questions offer several alternatives for your discussion. If you are a fairly prosperous group, you might at least briefly address the first "Optional Application" on page 152. Notice that God doesn't condemn prosperity (He offers it), but He warns against wrong attitudes about it. How does this fact apply to you?

Alternatively, you can use question 13 and some of Moses' images to discuss how God's nature is relevant to your lives. How have you known Him to be a rock, a refuge, a father, a mother, an avenger, or a discipliner in your lives? In what situations you are currently facing do you need to focus on one or another of these aspects of Him? How might you pray, act, or respond to Him in light of these aspects?

You might return to question 1 about fear. What

aspects of God's nature specifically encourage you to grow less afraid instead of burying or denying your fears?

Prayer. Praise God for His nature and thank Him for the ways in which you experience Him. Ask Him to guard you from fear, from self-confidence in prosperity, and from all other attitudes that dishonor Him. Ask Him for the courage with which Moses faced death and Joshua faced the leadership of an invading army and clan.

Wrap-up. Alert members that at the beginning of your next meeting you will ask them to describe one way in which they experienced the Lord as Rock, Father, or another of the images you discussed.

Optional lessons. If you didn't do any of the optional lessons after lesson 9, this is a good time to do at least one. See the paragraphs on those lessons on pages 120 and 125.

1. Kenneth Barker, ed., The NIV Study Bible (Grand Rapids, MI: Zondervan, 1985), 281–282.
2. Barker, 281.
3. J. A. Thompson, *Deuteronomy: An Introduction and Commentary* (London: InterVarsity, 1974), 305–306.
4. Barker, 287.

LESSON THIRTEEN

REVIEW

*"These commandments that I give you today are
to be upon your hearts. . . . Talk about them when
you sit at home and when you walk along the road,
when you lie down and when you get up."*
Deuteronomy 6:6-7

After so many weeks, Deuteronomy may be a jumble
in your mind. This is your opportunity to pull it all
together so that its key points are yours forever.

You may want to leaf through the past twelve
lessons before or during this review. Ask God to
remind you of what He would like you to remember.

1. Think about what Deuteronomy as a whole is
   about. Then write your own title for the book
   and subtitles for each of its main divisions.
   (Change the divisions given if you like.)

   Deuteronomy: _____

   _____

   1:1–3:29 _____

   _____

   4:1–11:32 _____

   _____

   12:1–26:19 _____

   _____

27:1–30:20 _____

_____

31:1–34:12 _____

_____

2. Why did Moses structure Deuteronomy like a Near Eastern treaty (covenant)?

_____

_____

_____

_____

_____

_____

3. In your own words, summarize the terms of the covenant between the Lord and Israel.

   a. What did the Lord promise to be and do for Israel (see 7:6-10,11-15,21-24; 8:5; 30:20)?

   _____

   _____

   _____

   _____

   _____

   b. What was Israel expected to be and do for the Lord (see 6:4-5; 7:6; 10:12-13)?

   _____

   _____

   _____

   _____

4. To answer the following two questions, refer back to previous lessons. If you can't answer them, keep them in mind as you study the New

Testament in the future. Some relevant passages are Romans 3:21-31; 8:1-39; 10:1-11; 12:1–13:14; Galatians 2:15–5:26.

a. In what ways does question 3 describe our relationship to God under the new covenant?

_____

_____

_____

_____

_____

_____

b. How is the new covenant different from the old?

_____

_____

_____

_____

_____

_____

5. According to Deuteronomy, what were the Lord's motives in making this covenant? For instance, was He responding to anything Israel had done (see 7:6-8; 9:6; 10:15)?

_____

_____

_____

_____

_____

For Thought and Discussion: What important truths of the gospel (about God, righteousness, salvation, love, sin, suffering, and so on) are missing from Deuteronomy?

For Thought and Discussion: Does the Old Testament relationship between obedience and prosperity apply to Christians (see Romans 4:4-8; 7:1-6; 8:1-4; Galatians 3:10-14; 6:7-8)? If so, how? If not, why not?

_____

_____

_____

6. What were supposed to be the people's motives for keeping their side of the relationship (see 4:6-8; 5:6; 6:20-25; 10:12-22; 30:20)?

_____

_____

_____

_____

_____

_____

7. Put a star by each of the motives you wrote in question 6 that should move you to love and obey the Lord. If you have other motivations as well, write them down.

_____

_____

_____

_____

_____

8. Explain the relationship between obedience and prosperity that Moses taught. (For example, did Israel earn prosperity?) See 4:40; 8:17-20; 28:1-2,15.

_____

_____

_____

_____

_____

158

9. How does Deuteronomy show why the sacrificial
   system of Leviticus (and its fulfillment in Christ)
   was necessary (see Deuteronomy 27:26; 30:6;
   Romans 3:19-26; 6:23)?

   _____

   _____

   _____

   _____

   _____

   _____

10. How did Deuteronomy fit into God's plan to save
    the world through the descendants of Abraham
    (see 7:6; 9:5; 30:1-9)? (You might ask someone
    knowledgeable or keep this question in mind for
    future study.)

   _____

   _____

   _____

   _____

   _____

   _____

11. List some aspects of God's character that
    Deuteronomy reveals, and tell one way in which
    it shows each aspect.

   _____

   _____

   _____

   _____

   _____

_____

_____

_____

_____

12. What did you learn about justice from Deuteronomy? (To answer, think about the Ten Commandments and any laws you studied from chapters 12–26. Come back to this question later if you have not yet looked at the optional lessons.)

_____

_____

_____

_____

_____

_____

_____

13. Are there any other themes from Deuteronomy that you want to remember? If so, what are they?

_____

_____

_____

_____

_____

14. Look back at the questions about the book that you may have listed at the end of each lesson. Has your study answered these questions? If not, do any of the questions still seem important to you? If you do still have significant questions, consider possible ways of further study on your

own or with someone who could help you to resolve these questions. Some of the sources on pages 216–220 may help you.

_____

_____

_____

_____

_____

15. Have you noticed any ways (thoughts, attitudes, opinions, behavior) in which you have changed as a result of studying Deuteronomy? If so, describe how you have changed.

_____

_____

_____

_____

_____

_____

16. Look back over the entire study at questions in which you expressed a desire to make some specific application. Has your study of Deuteronomy pointed out a need to pursue further growth in some aspect of your walk with the Lord? If so, consider how you might start and then keep going. Pray about this, and write any notes here.

_____

_____

_____

_____

For the group

As a warm-up, give everyone a chance to share how he or she experienced God this week in one of the ways you discussed at your last meeting. Then you can probably just follow the rest of the lesson as it is. At the end, you might plan another meeting to make plans for the future. Some questions you might discuss are:

What did you learn about small-group study?

How well did the study help you grasp the book of Deuteronomy?

What were the most important truths you discovered together about the Lord?

What did you like best about your meetings?

What did you like least? What would you change?

How well did you meet the goals you set at your first meeting?

What are the members' current needs?

What will you do next?

1. J. Sidlow Baxter, *Explore the Book* (Grand Rapids, MI: Zondervan, 1966), 212.

DEUTERONOMY 12:1-32

Pure Worship

"Be careful not to be ensnared by inquiring about their gods, saying, 'How do these nations serve their gods? We will do the same.'"
Deuteronomy 12:30

When the Israelites moved into Canaan, they found cities of people who by comparison were wealthy and sophisticated. The Canaanites' values and beliefs were a lot like the ones most Israelites had had in Egypt. So they were naturally tempted to copy their new neighbors, or at least join with them occasionally just to be sociable. But God wanted Israel to be in Canaan but not of it; He wanted Israel to be pure.

   In some ways, our position as Christians in an unbelieving world is much like Israel's (see 1 Peter 2:11). As you study chapter 12, ask yourself what you can learn about God's character and commands that applies to us and what commands applied only to Israel.

1. Much of the legal section of Deuteronomy lacks obvious structure, but roughly the first third of the section (chapters 12–16) discusses the proper way to worship the Lord. Why do you suppose Moses addressed right worship first and at such length?

2. Read 12:1-32, preferably more than once. You will notice that Moses repeats himself for emphasis. However, what main commands is he trying to get across?

For Thought and Discussion: Do you think 12:2-3 applies to Christians in any way, or was it meant just for Israel's unique situation? If you think it applies to us, does it apply just to our inner spiritual warfare or also to our dealings with unbelievers? How do you think it applies, or why do you think it doesn't? Pray about this, and support your opinion from Scripture.

For Thought and Discussion: Some groups believe that it is wrong to keep any custom with pagan origins or any holiday not commanded in the Bible. Following are listed some symbols and customs that have pagan origins. For each, explain why you think Christians should reject it, use it, or use it with some changes.
- Christmas tree
- Santa Claus
- Christmas on December 25
- Easter Bunny
- Halloween

Destroy completely (12:2-3)

3. One main command is "Destroy completely all the places . . . where the nations you are dispossessing worship their gods" (12:2-3). Why was this essential (see 4:24; 5:6-10; 6:4; 7:6; 9:5; 12:31)?

The place the Lord will choose

(12:4-14,29-31)

4. What do you observe from chapter 12 about how the Canaanites worshiped their gods (see 12:2-3,31)?

Detestable things (12:31). See the boxes called "Canaanite Religion" on pages 100 and 169.

---

5. The Lord commanded, "You must not worship the LORD your God in their way" (12:4). Why was it wrong to worship the Lord as the pagans worshiped (see Deuteronomy 4:15; 12:31; Leviticus 11:44-45)?

Ensnared (12:30). The temptation upon Israel to conform was intense. Canaan's gods offered fertility and power, the two things everyone wanted most. Worshiping with their neighbors won the Israelites acceptance into a sophisticated culture, business and social contacts, and an alternative to constant hostility. In fact, from the death of Joshua onward, these temptations proved irresistible to most Israelites and eventually led to the nation's destruction.

---

6. a. What are some of the "gods" of the non-Christians in your community, workplace, and society?

   b. What are some ways in which your neighbors

164

worship their gods? (Think about the sacrifices they make, the ways they use their money, the special days they observe, the rituals they practice.)

c. Are you tempted in any ways to participate in the ungodly goals and practices you just mentioned? If so, what tempts you, and what practical steps can you take to resist this temptation?

The place the LORD your God will choose (12:5). During the desert journey, Israel's worship centered around the *tabernacle* ("dwelling place").[1] This tent housed the ark of the covenant, the altar of sacrifice, and the other articles of Israel's worship (see Exodus 25:1–27:21). The tabernacle was the sanctuary ("holy place") where God dwelt among His people (see Exodus 25:8; compare John 1:14 and Revelation 21:3). In the desert, the tribes of Israel always camped around the tabernacle.

When Israel entered Canaan, the people would no longer all live gathered around the tabernacle but would scatter across the land. The Lord would choose one city where the tabernacle would be set up. To this central sanctuary the Israelites would gather three times a year (see Deuteronomy 16:16) for the great holy days of their faith. They would also gather there to seek the Lord's will for joint projects, such as war. This periodic gathering at a common worship center would keep Israel from disintegrating into self-interested tribes and clans; the Lord wanted His people to become a single nation, united in His service. The more each family and clan did as it saw fit in its own region, the more likely the people were to drift into pagan ways and forget their ties to Israelites from other tribes. The book of Judges shows that this is just what happened.

The books of Joshua, Judges, and Samuel mention authorized sacrifices at places other than the tabernacle at Shiloh. It may be that except for the main festivals three times a year, authorized priests were permitted to sacrifice at certain other sites (see Deuteronomy 27:6-7; Joshua 8:30-31; 1 Samuel 7:5-9). The goal of Deuteronomy 12:4-14 was to limit the number

Optional Application: Do you know someone who is suffering temptation to conform to the world's ways of worship? If so, how can you help him or her? Begin with persistent prayer.

For Thought and Discussion: a. To what extent can we Christians worship as we see fit, and to what extent do we need to conform to standards for the same reasons that Israel did (consider 1 Corinthians 14:26-40)?

b. Where is God's dwelling place now (see 1 Corinthians 3:16; 6:19; Ephesians 2:22; 1 Peter 2:5)?

165

For Thought and Discussion: Compare what you wrote in questions 9 and 10 to the attitudes behind Canaanite worship and/or the attitudes that dominate your society.

of authorized altars and encourage the people to gather as a nation to worship.[2]

7. What can we learn from 12:1-14 about the Lord's character, priorities, and desires for His people that still applies today?

Burnt offerings (12:6). See the box "Sacrifices: Old Testament Grace" on page 90.

Sacrifices (12:6). This Hebrew word specifies offerings in thanks to God and for fellowship with Him (see "fellowship offering" on page 91). Such sacrifices included verbal praise and thanks, **freewill offerings**, and **what you have vowed to give** ("votive offerings" in RSV, NASB; see Deuteronomy 23:21-23). The priest, the offerer, and the Lord each had a share in these sacrifices.

Tithes (12:6). These were percentages of one's harvest of grapes, oil, grain, and herds (Deuteronomy 14:22-29, 15:19-23). **Special gifts** (NASB: "the contribution of your hand"; RSV: "the offering that you present"; KJV: "heave offerings") were the portion of the tithes that supported the priests.[3]

Levites (12:12). See page 184.

8. Instead of worshiping as the Canaanites did or however they saw fit, the Israelites were supposed to do certain acts of worship. What kinds of worship does Moses name?

12:6

12:7,12

9. What attitudes toward God do you think these acts of worship expressed?

10. What attitudes about fellow worshipers were important (see 12:12,18-19)?

166

11. Put a star beside each attitude you named in questions 9 and 10 that a Christian should express in worship. Then write down at least one specific way you could express or encourage one of those attitudes in your own (private or corporate) worship.

Holy and common (12:15-28)

Ceremonially unclean (12:15). This is a religious distinction, not a moral one; an unclean person was temporarily barred from touching holy things or approaching the Holy God through sacrifice. A person became unclean by touching objects that symbolized earthly life: dead bodies, menstrual blood, semen, and so on (see Leviticus 11:1–15:33). To pagans, these substances enabled a person to tap the power of the world's god-forces, but the Lord wanted to impress upon Israel the distinction between Himself and the physical life He had created. He did not want to be confused with or worshiped like the Canaanite god Baal. Although earthly substances were not in themselves more evil or corrupt than spiritual substances, the Lord made a separation to teach the distinction between the created power of earth and the Holy Creator of heaven and earth.

Consecrated (12:26). Set apart for holy purpose. The distinction between created life and the Creator was a distinction between the common and the holy. Anything that belonged to God or was used for relating to Him (offerings, priests, and so on) was on a different plane from ordinary earthly things. The Lord stressed the distinction between holy and common in most areas of life (see Leviticus 10:10), including separating holy days from ordinary days (see Deuteronomy 5:12) and consecrated meat from ordinary meat (see Deuteronomy 12:15-27).

12. From Deuteronomy 12:4,23 and from what page 169 tells you about Canaanite practices, explain why the Lord forbade His people to eat blood (see 12:16,23-25,27).

167

For Thought and
Discussion: Is the
distinction between
holy and common
relevant to our lives in
any ways? If so, how?
If not, why not?

Optional
Application: Choose
a key verse to
meditate on, such as
verse 4, 7, 18, 23, or 31.

13. The blood of consecrated meat was poured
beside the altar, and the meat had to be eaten at
the holy place by ceremonially clean worshipers
(see 12:17-18,26-27). By contrast, the blood of
ordinary meat was poured on ordinary ground,
and the meat could be eaten anywhere by
anyone (see 12:15,20-25).
    What did Israel learn about God and the
world from the distinction between holy and
common?

14. How would you summarize in a sentence the
message of 12:1-32?

15. List any questions you have about chapter 12.

For the group

Warm-up. Ask, "When you first became serious
about being a Christian, what was the hardest area
of your life to let go of or change?"

Discussion. Try to draw out the main principles
that chapter 12 teaches, such as "Do not worship as
the Canaanites worship." You can discuss specific
laws under each principle if you like, but focus on
the *reasons* behind each principle. Look at the chapter in the light of the Ten Commandments, God's
plan for His people, and God's character. Then discuss how each principle applies to the Christian life.
    After you discuss ways your culture tempts
you to accept its gods (its goals and values) and its
means of worship (its rituals and works), you might
pray for each person in the group. Ask for God's
strength daily to resist temptation. How can you
encourage one another? What can you learn from
each other's struggles?
    If the group has trouble recognizing its cul-
ture's gods, ask, "What is the god of the secular
humanist? Of the Marxist? Of the radical feminist?
Of the upwardly mobile capitalist? Of the overzeal-
ous patriot? You may stir up the emotions of group
members who rightly insist that some reverence for
man, woman, liberty, equality, prosperity, pleasure,
health, life, one's country, one's family, the earth,
and so on is appropriate. Help the group recognize
when appropriate reverence becomes inappropriate
worship.

Regarding rituals, consider Christmas, Thanksgiving, Easter, and Halloween as practiced by non-Christians. Consider secular holidays and major annual sporting events. Think about how people pursue hobbies, health, dieting, beauty, fame, and financial success.

Prayer. Praise God for His holiness. Meditate together on the reasons He alone is worthy of worship.

Canaanite Religion, Part 2

Sun, rain, and fertility were unpredictable in Canaan, so religion's chief goal was to influence the divine forces of nature to give these in desirable times and amounts. The primary method of attempting to tap the gods' power was "sympathetic magic." That is, the Canaanites acted out rituals that they wanted their deities to imitate.

For instance, men performed sex acts with women holy to Baal so that Baal would water the earth. Rites with menstrual blood tapped Astarte's fertility for the land. The blood of sacrificed animals was eaten or sprinkled on the earth because the blood carried the power of life (see Genesis 9:4; Leviticus 17:10-14; Deuteronomy 12:23). Substances that symbolized the great forces of life—dead bodies, blood, semen—were frequently used in religious magic.[4]

Animals and crops were offered to the gods for various reasons. Sacrifices could purchase a god's favor in war, for the gods were not naturally faithful to humans (see 2 Kings 3:26-27; 16:2-3). Sacrifice "brought the worshiper into sympathy and rhythm with the physical world"[5]—this was necessary for sympathetic magic. Finally, the gods supposedly needed food and drink just like people (see Isaiah 57:5-6; Jeremiah 7:18).

---

1. Kenneth Barker, ed., *The NIV Study Bible* (Grand Rapids, MI: Zondervan, 1985), 123.
2. J. A. Thompson, *Deuteronomy: An Introduction and Commentary* (London: InterVarsity, 1974), 162–164; Craigie, 217.
3. Thompson, 167–168.
4. Peter C. Craigie, *The Book of Deuteronomy* (Grand Rapids, MI: Eerdmans, 1976), 132.
5. Packer, Tenney, and White, 107. See also 161–180.

DEUTERONOMY 13:1-18; 14:1-2; 16:21-22; 17:1-7; 18:9-22

Prophecy and Magic

"You shall have no other gods before me.'"
Deuteronomy 5:7

"You are a people holy to the LORD your God. Out of all the peoples on the face of the earth, the LORD has chosen you to be his treasured possession."
Deuteronomy 14:2

Knowledge is power. The more we know, the more we feel in control of what will happen to us. Maybe that's why magic, prophecy, and the occult attracted Israel: The pagan gods seemed so much more generous with information and power than the Lord, who would tell only what He chose, when He chose, and through means He chose. But the security of knowing what the Lord doesn't want to tell is an illusion. No amount of knowledge will ever really give the control we crave.

This lesson deals with permitted and forbidden ways of attaining knowledge and control over life. Feel free to cover only a few of the passages since the lesson is long. Ask God to help you find and apply what is relevant to your life.

Forbidden knowledge (18:9-14)

1. What kinds of practices did the Lord forbid (see 18:9-11)?

171

For Thought and Discussion: How do people wrongly seek knowledge and control in your day?

For Further Study: Contrast Molech-worship to the worship of the Lord described in Micah 6:6-8. How can you apply this to your own life? What sacrifices does God ask of you?

Sacrifices his son or daughter in the fire (18:10). Literally, "makes . . . pass through the fire." This may have been a magic test or trial by ordeal, or it may have been human sacrifice; in either case, it was an offering to the god Molech (see Leviticus 18:21; 2 Kings 23:10; Jeremiah 32:35).

The Phoenicians, who entered Canaan shortly after Israel did, used an idol of Molech with a human body and a bull's head. "The image of metal was heated red hot by a fire kindled within, and the children laid on its arms rolled off into the fiery pit below. In order to drown the cries of the victims, flutes were played, and drums were beaten; and mothers stood by without tears or sobs, to give the impression of the voluntary character of the offering."[1]

Israel shared with the Phoenicians the idea that the best of everything, including the firstborn of man and beast, belonged to God (see Exodus 13:11-16; Numbers 3:40-51). However, God told Israel to redeem each firstborn human with a ransom price so that the person would glorify God by his life, not his death (compare Romans 12:1).

Divination (18:10). This word covers various magical ways of discerning the gods' will. For instance, in Ezekiel 21:21, the word names the practice of whirling arrows and deciding "yes" or "no" according to which arrow is thrown out.[2]

Sorcery (18:10). "Witchcraft" in NASB; "observer of times" in KJV; "soothsayer" in RSV. This is either one who divines the future by reading clouds or one who performs incantations.[2]

Interprets omens (18:10). "Enchanter" in KJV; "augur" in RSV. This is one who discerns secrets or the future by reading reflections in a cup (see Genesis 44:5,15) or by watching birds, fire, rain, or other "natural phenomena."[2]

Witchcraft (18:10). "Sorcerer" in RSV, NASB. One who brews herbs for magic (see Micah 5:12).[2]

172

Casts spells (18:11). "Charmer" in KJV, RSV. Literally, "one who ties knots"—"one who binds another by magic knots or magic spells."[2]

Medium (18:11). "Consulter with familiar spirits" in KJV. This is someone who professes to call up the spirits of dead people for consultation (see 1 Samuel 28:11).[3]

Spiritist (18:11). "Wizard" in RSV, KJV. This may be a synonym for "medium," or it may be specifically someone who consults only a particular spirit. The familiar spirit is supposedly a dead person, but it may in fact be a demon or simply a fraud.[4]

Consults the dead (18:11). "Necromancer" in RSV, KJV. This may be a general term that covers "medium" and "spiritist": a person who performs magic and future-telling by communicating with the dead.[5]

Optional Application: Pray for someone you know who dabbles in astrology or other forbidden ways of acquiring knowledge and power. Ask God to enable that person to cut free from that involvement and turn to Him for security and importance.

2. From the definitions above, summarize the goals of these pursuits.

3. Why do you think these practices were "detestable" (18:12)? That is, how did both their *ends* and their *means* dishonor the Lord?

4. Many of these same (and similar) practices are still popular today. What can Christians do to help people who are involved in such pursuits?

True prophets (13:1-5; 18:15-22)

Prophet (18:15). One who is "called" by God. A parallel term is seer, one who "sees" the truth in events and "sees" the mind of God because of intimate relationship with Him.[6]

In all the Torah, only Deuteronomy 18:15-19 mentions the office of the Lord's prophet. Moses refers to the line of prophets who will follow him, although many centuries later, Jews began to await one Prophet, the Messiah, who would free them as Moses had done.

For Further Study:
Explore the role of a prophet in Israel by studying one of the prophetic books, or the career of Elijah (see 1 Kings 17:1– 2 Kings 2:11) or Elisha (see 1 Kings 19:19– 2 Kings 13:21).

For Thought and Discussion: Did 18:22 mean that the people were supposed to wait until the prophet's prediction (of judgment, for instance) had come true before they listened to his warning? If not, what might God have meant?

For Thought and Discussion: Why couldn't Israel be sure that a prophet was from the Lord just because his prediction came true? How does 13:1-3 balance 18:21-22?

For Further Study:
Study the prophet's role in the New Testament church, in such passages as Ephesians 4:11-13, Acts 11:27-30, and Acts 21:10-14.

5. One reason Israel didn't need to pursue knowledge in forbidden ways was that God had given His Word in the Torah. What was another reason (see 18:14-18)?

6. Why did Israel need prophets (see 18:16)? (Compare 5:23-31.)

7. Ezekiel further described a prophet's role when he prophesied against false prophets. What did he say a prophet should do?

   Ezekiel 13:3-5
   Ezekiel 22:30-31 (Compare Psalm 106:23.)

8. Summarize in your own words what a prophet was supposed to be and do.

9. Of course, anyone might (and did) claim to speak God's Word. How was Israel to know whether a prophet really spoke for God?

   Deuteronomy 13:1-3
   Deuteronomy 18:21-22

10. What was Israel supposed to do to false prophets (see 13:5; 18:20)?

11. The Lord condemned anyone who said, "The Lord says . . ." when he was really giving his sincere opinion about what to do (see 18:20). Does this have any application to our own day? If so, what? If not, why not?

The last Old Testament prophet was Malachi, in the mid 400s. The Lord was apparently silent for almost five hundred years, until the true last prophet of the old covenant and herald of the new—John the Baptist—began to preach.

At Pentecost, the Holy Spirit, whom the Lord had previously given only to prophets, was poured out upon all believers. From then on, a prophet's intimacy with God was available to all Christians (see Joel 2:28-29; Acts 2:14-21). Nevertheless, the New Testament church recognized prophets in its midst (see Matthew 10:41; Ephesians 4:11; 1 Corinthians 12:28; Acts 11:27; 21:10).

12. When someone claims to be proclaiming God's

current instructions for His people, how do you think Christians should verify his words? Use Scripture to show why your method is valid. (For example, see Deuteronomy 13:1-3; 18:21-22; Matthew 7:15-23; Galatians 1:8-9; 1 John 4:1-3.)

For Thought and Discussion: Does 13:6-18 have any lessons for Christians? Why or why not?

For Further Study: Why did Moses want Israel to "be afraid" (13:11) when they saw the seducer's fate?

Secret seducer's (13:6-18)

A false prophet spoke for other gods or claimed falsely to speak for the Lord. He was to be executed (see 13:5; 18:20) because he preached open rebellion against Israel's Savior and Redeemer (see 13:5). The same penalty was prescribed for anyone who seduced people to secret idolatry.

13. a. With what attitude was a person supposed to denounce a seducer (see 13:8-9)?

b. Why do you think God expected this attitude?

14. a. If any people heard of idolatry in another town, what were they supposed to do first (see 13:12-14)?

b. Is this relevant today? Why or why not?

Whole burnt offering (13:16). Recall from page 91 what this was.

---

15. Why would an idolatrous town become "a whole burnt offering to the LORD" (13:15-18)?

16. What can we learn about the Lord's character from 13:6-18 and the other passages in this lesson?

Other detestable acts

(14:1-2; 16:21-22; 17:1)

Cut yourselves or shave . . . (14:1). These were rites for mourning the dead that Canaanites practiced. Those people evidently believed that

175

with magic they could persuade the dead to do things for the living.[7]

17. In your own words, explain what was wrong with each of the following acts:

mourning the dead in pagan ways (14:1-2). (See 12:29-31.)

setting up a pagan idol beside the Lord's altar (16:21-22). (See 5:6-10.)

sacrificing a flawed animal (17:1). (See Malachi 1:6-8.)

18. Are Christians ever tempted to hold on to customs that conflict with Christian faith or to offer God less-than-perfect sacrifices (see Romans 12:1-2)? If so, name at least one way we can be tempted to do this.

19. a. What is the most significant thing you have learned from studying the passages in this lesson?

b. How can you act on what you have learned in some specific way?

20. List any questions you have about this lesson.

For the group

Warm-up. Since this study is about wrong and right sources of knowledge and power, you might begin by asking members to each name one piece of information he or she would really like to know if it were possible.

Read aloud. Select those passages you find interesting. Don't feel obliged to cover all the passages in this lesson.

Summarize the main message or purpose of the passages.

Questions. Focus on the lessons God was teaching Israel through these laws. The Scripture doesn't always say, "This law should teach you that . . . ," so you will need to do some thinking. What do you learn about God and holiness (dedication to God) from these passages? Why does God forbid some ways of seeking knowledge? Anyone in your group who has had experience with the occult should be able to answer this question from personal experience. However, Deuteronomy 5:7 and other passages should also be clues.

Many Christians feel that the office of prophet no longer exists now that we have the New Testament. Yet we still have leaders who claim to speak God's will for specific situations, even if they do not claim direct divine inspiration. Therefore, question 12 is a timely issue. Try to spend most of your time on that and other application questions.

Prayer.

1. T. Nicol, "Molech, Moloch," *The International Standard Bible Encyclopedia*, vol. 3, ed. James Orr (Grand Rapids, MI: Eerdmans, 1956), 2074–2075.
2. J. A. Thompson, *Deuteronomy: An Introduction and Commentary* (London: InterVarsity, 1974), 211.
3. Thompson, 212.
4. Thompson, 212.
5. Thompson, 212.
6. C. H. Peisker, "Prophet," *The New International Dictionary of New Testament Theology*, vol. 3, ed. Colin Brown (Grand Rapids, MI: Zondervan, 1978), 77.
7. Peter C. Craigie, *The Book of Deuteronomy* (Grand Rapids, MI: Eerdmans, 1976), 229–230.

DEUTERONOMY 14:1-21; 16:1-17

Ceremonies of Holiness

*"You are a people holy to the L*ORD *your God."*
Deuteronomy 14:2

We celebrate to relive an event, to remember
what it means to us. Our celebrations—Easter,
Thanksgiving, Christmas—show what is important
to us about life and God. The new covenant came
with new events to celebrate that replaced Israel's
festivals, but the old ones still echo through the
New Testament and show us facets of God we might
otherwise forget.

Dietary laws (14:3-21)

Read 14:3-21 carefully. Look for the overall point
of the passage and for the key words that show this
point.

Unclean (14:8). The word suggests "sin and defile-
ment"[1] rather than mere unhealthiness.
Touching blood, dead bodies, and bodily dis-
charges produced a temporary uncleanness that
kept a person away from society and sacrifice,
but eating unclean food was *detestable* (see
14:3).
The Lord's reasons for declaring a given
animal unclean for food are not always
evident. However, we can see some patterns
with the little we know of the ancient world.

179

Some forbidden animals (such as pigs and carrion fowl) often carried disease. Some were "foolishly uneconomical to raise as food"[2] in that part of the world. Some were favored for animal sacrifices and cultic meals by pagan groups. And some were frequent sources of food allergies.[3] Explanations are uncertain partly because scholars disagree about just what animal many of the Hebrew words in 14:3-21 refer to.

Do not cook . . . in its mother's milk (14:21). Scholars have thought that this command prohibited a Canaanite magical practice. Recently, however, the Canaanite text on which this theory rests has been retranslated so that it no longer supports this theory. Many scholars now follow an older understanding of 14:21.

Milk is a life-giving and life-representing substance for an infant animal. The Old Testament Law consistently separates holy from common, clean from unclean, and life from death. From this point of view, it would be scandalous to let the source of a young animal's life (milk) become the source of its death in cooking.[4]

Keep in mind this principle of separation as you try to understand other laws.

---

1. God designated some foods as clean and others as "detestable" (14:3) because "you are a people holy to the LORD your God" (14:2,21). Read the definitions of "unclean" and "consecrated" on pages 167 and 179. What could the distinction between clean and unclean have taught Israel about holiness?

2. God forbade Israel to eat foods that the Canaanites ate both for religious rites and ordinary meals. How would these laws have helped Israel to become a holy nation, separate from pagan peoples?

The early Christians decided the new covenant did not require Gentiles to keep the dietary laws, although Jewish Christians were free to keep them if they liked (see Acts 10:9-15; 15:1-29; Romans 14:1-4,14).

3. From the following cross-references, write what God was teaching Christians by not requiring the dietary laws in the new covenant.

   Acts 11:1-18 (Read 10:1-48 if necessary.)

   Matthew 15:11,17-20 (Jesus was speaking of a law about washing, but His words apply equally to the Jews' mistaken understanding of the dietary laws' purpose.)

   Colossians 2:13-23

For Further Study:
a. Study one of the Gospels (such as Mark 14:1–15:47) for connections between the Passover and Jesus' Passion.
   b. Study other references to the Passover in the Gospels, such as John 2:13–3:26 or 5:1–6:71.

In Deuteronomy 16, Moses reminded Israel of the three major festivals the people were supposed to keep each year. He dated the feasts only loosely to correspond to agricultural events. He gave precise dates in the priestly handbook, Leviticus (see 23:24).

It isn't surprising that the Lord wanted Israel's major festivals to celebrate His role in agriculture. Not only would agriculture be Israel's primary day-to-day issue, but it was also the focus of the pagan religions competing for Israel's loyalty. (See the box Canaanite Religion" on page 169.) At the same times of year when the Canaanites held festivals to induce the gods to grant fertility, Israel held festivals to honor the Lord for His works. By this means, Israel remained the Lord's holy people, separate from the pagans.[5]

Passover (16:1-8)

At the place the LORD will choose (see 16:2). See page 165.

---

4. Briefly describe the event that the Passover recalls (see Exodus 12:1-39).

Sacrifice (16:2). On the eve of Passover, unblemished lambs or goats were killed by the priests, roasted, and eaten by the gathered families. The animals signified that blood had been shed in place of the Israelites blood to purchase their freedom from judgment.

ISRAEL'S FEASTS

number	month Hebrew name	modern equivalent	agriculture	feast
1	Abib (Nisan after the Babylonian captivity)	March–April	Spring rains, barley and flax harvest	Passover Abib 14 Unleavened Bread Abib 15–21 Firstfruits Abib 16 (Leviticus 23:9-14)
2	Ziv (Iyyar)	April–May	Barley harvest	
3	Sivan	May–June	Wheat harvest	Weeks (Pentecost, Harvest, Firstfruits [Numbers 28:26, KJV]) Sivan 6
4	Tammuz	June–July		
5	Ab	July–August		
6	Elul	August–September		
7	Ethanim (Tishri)	September–October	Autumn rains begin; plowing	Trumpets Tishri 1 Day of Atonement Tishri 10 Tabernacles (Booths) Tishri 15–21 Sacred Assembly Tishri 22
8	Bul	October–November		
9	Kislev	November–December		
10	Tebeth	December–January		
11	Shebat	January–February		
12	Adar	February–March		Purim Adar 14–15

Adapted from "Hebrew calendar and selected events" and "Old Testament feasts and other sacred days," *The NIV Study Bible*, 102–103, 176–177.

5. Paul called Christ "our Passover lamb" (1 Corinthians 5:7). How does the Passover shed light on what Jesus has done for us (see Exodus 12:7,12-13; Isaiah 53:4-12; John 1:29)?

Unleavened bread (16:3). This was common among nomads because it was quick to prepare. Settled peoples usually preferred leavened bread.

---

6. Why did Israel eat unleavened bread for Passover (see 16:3)?

7. In 1 Corinthians 5:7-8, Paul explains the meaning of purging the house from yeast for seven days (see Deuteronomy 16:4). What did the yeast represent, and what did purging the house of it mean?

The Feast of Weeks (16:9-12)

The feasts of Passover and Unleavened Bread (see Deuteronomy 16:8; Leviticus 23:4-8) were held at the barley harvest. Depending on the weather, the wheat harvest ended about seven weeks later. Exodus 23:16 calls the feast at that time the Feast of Harvest; Numbers 28:26 (KJV) calls it the Day of Firstfruits; Deuteronomy calls it the Feast of Weeks.

In Jesus' day, the Jews scheduled this feast by counting seven Sabbaths from the Passover and holding the Feast of Weeks on the following Sunday. Greek-speaking Jews called the feast *Pentecost* (*pente koste* means "fiftieth day") because the seven weeks plus one day equaled fifty days.

8. What did the Feast of Weeks celebrate (see Deuteronomy 16:10)?

9. How did Israel celebrate this feast (see Deuteronomy 16:10-11)?

10. Is Israel's manner of celebrating holy days (holidays) an example for us in any ways? If so, how?

Optional Application: Read Luke 12:1 and 1 Corinthians 5:7-8. Do you need to purge your life of any leaven? If so, specifically what do you need to do?

For Further Study: Study the New Testament event that occurred at the Feast of Weeks (see Acts 2).

For Further Study:
Jesus fulfilled the
Feast of Tabernacles
just as He fulfilled the
Passover. How did
He do this? John 1:14
is literally "The Word
became flesh and
tabernacled among
us" (see also John
14:23; Revelation 21:3).

For Further Study:
John 7:14–8:59
records events at one
Feast of Tabernacles
in Jerusalem. Read
John 7:37-39. Think
about the events the
Jews were reliving,
camping in tents
on the rooftops
of Jerusalem. Why
was this occasion
appropriate for what
Jesus did?

The Feast of Tabernacles (16:13-17)

Tabernacles (16:13). A tabernacle was the tent in
which a nomad lived. The Israelites had been
living in tabernacles since the Exodus, but their
children would live in houses in the Promised
Land. The tent that held the ark of the covenant
and symbolized the Lord tenting among His
people was also called a tabernacle (see Exodus
25:8-9). The same word is translated "booths"
in Leviticus 23:42-43.

*For seven days after you have gathered the
produce of your threshing floor and your
winepress* (16:13). In September or October,
depending on the harvest. This feast is called
the Feast of Ingathering in Exodus 23:16; 34:22.
Read Leviticus 23:39-43 to see what Israel did
during the Feast of Tabernacles.

11. What aspects of this celebration did Moses stress
in his sermon (see Deuteronomy 16:14-15)?

12. Explain the meanings of the feast (see
Deuteronomy 16:15; Leviticus 23:43).

Levites (16:11). They were originally one of the
twelve tribes of Israel, but the Lord set them
apart to care for the tabernacle (later the
Temple) and to do all the work connected with
the sacrificial system (see Numbers 3:5-13). One
family, the sons of Aaron, were the priests who
actually performed the sacrifices, and the rest
of the Levites prepared animals, cleaned up, and
so on. Every tribe was allotted land in Canaan
except the Levites, for they were dedicated to
God. However, God foresaw that there would be
more Levites than the tabernacle work would
require, so He required Israel to take care of
those who lived in villages but owned no land.
Apparently, these extra Levites became the
teachers, health inspectors, clerks, and other
professionals who needed more education than
farmers and craftsmen received.[6]

13. On slaves, see page 200. On aliens and widows, see page 121. Why was it so important to the Lord that His people include the disadvantaged in His feasts (see 16:11,14; 10:19)?

The Torah today

14. What can we learn about God from the three feasts Moses spoke about?

15. Does 14:1-21 or 16:1-17 have any practical implications for your life right now? If so, what are they, and how can you act on them?

16. List any questions you have about this study.

For the group

Warm-up. Ask group members to think of something they particularly like about a certain holiday or Christian celebration. Give everyone a chance to explain what about that celebration makes it so special.

Dietary Laws. First, try to understand what the laws were and what their purposes for Israel were. Then talk about why it is significant that these laws have been canceled for Christians. If group members have trouble understanding the point of the dietary laws, you might point out that the apostles told Gentile Christians not to eat blood and strangled animals because these were associated with pagan rituals (see Acts 15:29) and that Germanic Christians have never been comfortable with eating horsemeat because Germanic pagans used to favor horses for cultic meals.[7]

The Feasts. You might read about each feast in a Bible dictionary or commentary before your meeting. At the meeting, have members quickly summarize what happened at each celebration, then discuss what each meant in Israel, and then explore the light it sheds on Christ's work, God's nature, and Christian celebrations.

Prayer.

For Thought and Discussion: Think about Christian celebrations of the Lord's past acts and ongoing provision. Does Moses' sermon suggest any principles that Christians might adopt for their celebrations? If so, what are they?

For Thought and Discussion: Can Christians learn anything about prosperity from Israel's festivals?

185

1. Kenneth Barker, ed., *The NIV Study Bible* (Grand Rapids, MI: Zondervan, 1985), 159.
2. Gordon Fee and Douglas Stuart, *How to Read the Bible for All Its Worth* (Grand Rapids, MI: Zondervan, 1982), 145.
3. Fee and Stuart, 145.
4. Jacob Milgrom, "You Shall Not Boil a Kid in Its Mother's Milk," *Bible Review*, vol. 1, number 3 (Washington DC: Biblical Archaeology Society, 1985), 48–55.
5. The early Christians used the same methods to wean converts away from pagan rites. The feast of Jesus' birth was scheduled at the time of the Roman Saturnalia (December 25). All Saints' Eve (All Hallow Even, Hallowe'en) was meant to replace the pagan "old year's night," the night of witches, of the Celtic calendar. See "Saturnalia" and "Hallow-e'en in *The Oxford English Dictionary*.
6. Roland de Vaux, *Ancient Israel*, vol. 1 (New York: McGraw-Hill, 1965), 74, 155, 344, 349, 353.
7. H. R. Ellis Davidson, *Gods and Myths of the Viking Age* (New York: Bell, 1981), 122; Eric Oxenstierna, *The Norsemen* (Greenwich, CT: New York Graphic Society, 1965), 67–69, 256.

OPTIONAL LESSON D

DEUTERONOMY 14:22-29; 18:1-8; 23:19-20; 24:6, 10-18; 26:1-15

Tithes and Loans

"You shall give it to the Levite, the alien, the fatherless and the widow, so that they may eat in your towns and be satisfied."
Deuteronomy 26:12

It wasn't easy to make a living as a farmer in Israel. With mouths to feed and unpredictable weather, people might have been nervous about setting aside ten percent or more of their incomes for charity and celebration. However, knowing God intimately—His character, promises, and priorities—would have made these commands both reasonable and possible.

Read 14:22-29 and 26:1-15, looking less for the specific rules than for the values God's Law was instilling in His people. Notice that the tithe was used in some surprising ways.

First and second year tithes

(14:22-27; 26:1-11)

Tenth (14:22). In the Near East, a tenth was traditionally the king's share of produce or booty (see 1 Samuel 8:15,17),[1] so it was also the share customarily given to one's god (see Genesis 14:20; 28:22).[2] *Tithe* is an Old English word meaning "tenth."

At the place he will choose (14:23). The central sanctuary where the ark of the covenant was kept. See page 165.

For Thought and Discussion: The New Testament nowhere explicitly says Christians must tithe, but it does repeatedly exhort us to give generously to others. How do you decide how much to give and to whom to give it?

For Further Study: Observe in 18:1-8 how Israel supported its professionals in charge of worship.

For Thought and Discussion: What should motivate a Christian to give part of his income to God?

Optional Application: If you were to make a thank offering like that of 26:1-11, what confession would you declare? Write it down and maybe read it to a friend.

For Further Study: a. Compare Paul's views on giving (see 2 Corinthians 8:1–9:15) to what Deuteronomy says. What principles of giving still apply to Christians?
b. See Jesus' words on giving in Matthew 6:1-4; Luke 6:27-38; 12:22-34; 18:9-14.

1. What were the Israelites supposed to do with a tenth of their farm produce, according to 14:22-27?

2. Why do you suppose doing this would teach them "to revere the LORD your God always" (14:23)?

Numbers 18:21-29 suggests that the Israelites ate only part of the tithe at this annual festival and gave the rest of the tithe to the Levites.[3] (On the Levites, see page 184.)

Firstfruits (26:2). According to Leviticus 23:10, this was a sheaf of new grain. At the Feast of Firstfruits in April (Abib 16, see page 182), the head of each household carried a sheaf to the sanctuary and declared what Deuteronomy 26:3,5-10 states.

Wandering (26:5). The word also means "perishing."[4] **Aramean** refers to Abraham, or possibly all the patriarchs, who were nomadic shepherds from Aram (near the Euphrates River).

---

3. What acts of grace (God's unearned kindness) were recalled in the confession of faith the Israelite made with his offering (26:5-10)?

4. Why is it important to us that God's grace played a large role in the Old Testament faith?

5. The confession in 26:5-10 reveals the purpose of the tithe given to God. Why did Israel tithe?

Third year tithes (14:28-29; 26:12-15)

6. The people did as in 14:22-27 and 26:1-11 two out of every three years at the Feast of Firstfruits. What happened to the tithes in the third year (see 14:28-29)?

7. Why was this second use of the tithe important to God (see 10:18-19)?

188

In the third year, the Israelite left his tithe in his hometown and brought an oath to the sanctuary instead of his produce. Read in 26:12-14 what the Israelite swore.

For Thought and Discussion: Consider the promise God made to those who obeyed His command (see 14:29; 26:15). Why do you think blessing was connected with generosity?

Eaten . . . in mourning . . . offered . . . to the dead (26:14). These were Canaanite rites. They may have been offered to dead ancestors so that the dead would work for the good of the living. Or they may have been part of the rites of the gods Baal and Tammuz. At harvest time, those gods were worshiped by the offering of firstfruit, and the death and rebirth of Tammuz (in the fertility cycle) was recalled.

Tammuz is the Phoenician (Canaanite) name for the god called Dumuzu in Babylon. The Babylonian myth says he was slain by a boar (a symbol of winter). The goddess Ishtar (Astarte in Phoenicia) mourned for her lover and went to the underworld to deliver him from death. His return signifies the coming of spring after winter in one myth, or the coming of life-giving rains after the withering summer in another. Women mourned Tammuz' death in June (see Ezekiel 8:14), so the fourth month of Israel's calendar took his name (see page 180).[5]

Thus, in Deuteronomy 26:14, the Israelite swore that he had not used any of his firstfruits to participate in pagan fertility rites.

For Thought and Discussion: The Israelites were tempted to use part of their charity tithes for pagan rites to gain ongoing economic security (see 26:14). What might a Christian be tempted to do with his money rather than give it to God and the needy?

---

8. What attitudes (toward God, others, money, self) do 14:22-29 and 26:1-15 encourage?

9. What can we learn from these verses about God's character and priorities and about how we should live?

10. Is there some specific way in which you would like to respond to what you have learned about giving? If so, what is it?

Loans (23:19-20; 24:6-18)

Read 23:19-20 and 24:6-18 for the spirit God expected of borrowers and lenders. Think about the commandments: "Six days you shall labor and do all your work" and "You shall not steal."

Interest (23:19). John Calvin and others think interest was forbidden only on loans to poor Israelites, as in Exodus 22:25-27 and Leviticus 25:35-38.[6] There were no big businessmen in Israel, and most of the few merchants were aliens and foreigners.[7] Israelites rarely borrowed to finance a business venture or to buy large goods like houses. A man would borrow only if poverty left him no alternative, so a loan was emergency relief.[8] J. A. Thompson points out that "the rate of interest in the Near East was exorbitant," fifty percent in some places.[9]

If these facts are true, they suggest two alternate conclusions. God may have intended to forbid interest on emergency loans to the poor and to permit it on business loans, or He may have intended to forbid interest from the poor and to discourage business loans altogether.

Foreigner (23:20). Possibly, most loans to foreigners were for business purposes, whereas most loans to Israelites were for emergencies. Israel was commanded to care for poor resident aliens (see 10:19).

---

11. Why do you think the Lord forbade charging interest on emergency loans (see 23:19)?

Millstones (24:6). Most households ground grain daily for the day's needs. The grain was crushed between two round flat stones, the upper of which spun on a rod. Without two millstones, a family would have no bread.

A poor man had only one *cloak* (24:13), which served as bed as well as garment.

---

12. Although interest was forbidden, collateral (a pledge) was permitted (see 24:6,10-15,17-18).

190

What attitudes toward the other person and himself do you think the practice of collateral instilled . . .

in the lender?
in the borrower?

13. Why do you think each practice concerning collateral was forbidden?

24:6
24:10-11
24:12-13
24:17-18

The Torah today

14. What do the passages you studied in this lesson show you about God's priorities and values?

15. Do any of the uses of the tithe (or some portion of one's income) set an example for Christians? If you think so, how might you follow this example? (*Optional*: If you are unfamiliar with New Testament teaching on giving, see the "For Further Study" questions in this lesson.)

celebrating with one's household and anyone who can't afford to, before the Lord (see 26:11)

caring for the needy (see 14:28-29)

supporting those in charge of worship (see 18:3-5)

other (explain)

16. There have been several application questions in this lesson, but if you would like to plan one specific application for this week, write down your thoughts after prayerful consideration.

17. List any questions you have about this study.

For Thought and Discussion: Consider Deuteronomy 23:19 and Luke 6:30,34-36. Should Christians give to *everyone* who asks, even if the person may waste the money? Why or why not?

For Thought and Discussion: a. How might applying these principles for loans affect the poor in your day, psychologically and financially?
    b. What barriers to applying these methods do you see? Might they be overcome? How, or why not?

Optional Application: How can you adopt and reflect the attitudes toward the poor that 24:6-18 shows? Think of some specific steps you can take.

For Thought and Discussion: How do the practices of tithes and loans differ from modern ways of providing social services? Compare the attitudes behind and the results of each method.

Optional Application: Pray about the portion of your income you set aside for the Lord's uses. Write down any conclusions or ideas you get from that prayer.

For the group

Warm-up. Many people come to a discussion of tithing feeling vaguely guilty that they don't give as much as they think they should. This feeling may discourage them from studying these passages. Or it may encourage them to be defensive against or self-righteously defensive of the laws of tithing. Some Christians believe that the law of 10 percent is a rule for Christians, while others reject this idea.

So, because giving is an emotional issue for many, you might begin by letting members briefly air their emotions about giving. You could let members share the biggest obstacle against giving generously that they face (many children, medical bills, taxes, worry about the future, not feeling the church uses the money wisely). Or you could ask members to describe how their first experience of giving felt.

Tithes. Quickly clarify what Israel did with tithed wealth in each year. Then focus on the attitudes you think these laws were meant to instill, what you learned about God, and how Christians might go about deciding how much and to whom they should give. You might discuss what makes our situation different from Israel's (the tax structure, the cash economy, and so on). As leader, you might want to read 2 Corinthians 8–9 for Paul's guidelines on giving, and Luke 6:27-38 and Luke 12:22-34 for Jesus' teaching. Notice that Paul and Jesus deal with the fears and attitudes that keep us from being generous, not just with the outward action. Do the reasons Moses teaches for giving still apply to Christians?

The Law freed Israel from wrestling with some issues that Christians have to face. For instance, Moses specified 10 percent, but how much should you give? Moses said to spend the tithe on religious workers and the needy, but to whom specifically should you give, and how much to each? Don't try to pin down rules for the group, but do confront the group with the decisions each Christian must make.

If you try to outline principles of giving, encourage each member to come to his own convictions after prayerful consideration. You might even set aside time to pray about this. Be aware that most people's budgets won't stand sudden, drastic changes and that guilt is not the motive Jesus and Paul teach for giving.

192

A fun and encouraging exercise for the group might be the "Optional Application" on page 188—the confession of faith. Let each member take ten minutes to write his own confession, and then let those who would like to read theirs do so. The memory of God's providence is the basis for giving in Deuteronomy, and it may motivate your group.

Loans. Many people see a hidden political agenda in a discussion of the lending laws. As leader, you might ask yourself how your own political biases affect what you see in these laws. Try to look at them from a point of view different from your usual one. In your discussion, focus on the attitudes that the group thinks the lending laws were intended to teach people. Ask yourselves how those same attitudes could be encouraged in your country's economic system. Consider how you might teach those attitudes to your children or practice them yourselves.

Prayer.

1. Kenneth Barker, ed., *The NIV Study Bible* (Grand Rapids, MI: Zondervan, 1985), 27.
2. Barker, 49.
3. Barker, 263.
4. J. A. Thompson, *Deuteronomy: An Introduction and Commentary* (London: InterVarsity, 1974), 255.
5. H. Porter, "Tammuz," *The International Standard Bible Encyclopedia*, vol. 5, 2908; Barker, 1238; Thompson, 258. The rites of Dumuzu/Tammuz and Ishtar/Astarte spread around the ancient world under the names of Osiris and Isis, Adonis and Aphrodite, Attis and Atargatis.
6. Rousas John Rushdoony, *The Institutes of Biblical Law* (The Craig Press, 1973), 249; Barker, 1249.
7. Roland de Vaux, *Ancient Israel*, vol. 1 (New York: McGraw-Hill, 1965), 78; Thompson, 242.
8. Peter C. Craigie, *The Book of Deuteronomy* (Grand Rapids, MI: Eerdmans, 1976), 302.
9. Thompson, 242.

OPTIONAL LESSON E

DEUTERONOMY 15:1-18; 23:24-25; 24:14-15,19-22; 25:13-16

More Economics

"Remember that you were slaves in Egypt and the LORD your God redeemed you. That is why I give you this command today."
Deuteronomy 15:15

Like the previous lesson, this one examines how the Lord applied His general principles of how to treat people to the specific circumstances Israel was going to face. When you study these laws, keep in mind the commandments about work, stealing, and coveting in Deuteronomy 5:13-14,19,21 and the Great Commandment to love your neighbor. The specific applications that suited Israel may seem foreign to you, but look for the principles and attitudes the Lord might have been trying to teach.

The lesson is long, so you can omit some sections or divide the lesson in two.

1. As you study each of the laws in this lesson, observe what you learn about God's character and priorities.

Wages (24:14-15)

Hired man (24:14). Either a poor alien or an Israelite who had lost his land through debt. He might be hired by the day or the year (see Leviticus 25:50,53; Deuteronomy 24:15). He was not quite a slave, for he could quit and keep a family. But because he had no savings, any

For Further Study: See what Paul says to masters in Ephesians 6:9.

Optional Application: Do you ever take advantage of your employees? If so, what should you do?

195

For Thought and Discussion: a. What could a worker do if he felt he was being exploited but did not want to quit (see Deuteronomy 24:15; Psalm 57:1-11)?
b. Should Christians do this (see Matthew 5:43-47; 6:14-15)?

For Further Study: What does Paul say in 2 Thessalonians 3:6-15 about the command to work?

For Thought and Discussion: How could one implement a system like gleaning in a city or suburb?

misfortune might obligate him to sell himself.[1] Poor families often needed wages each day to pay for the next day's food and shelter.

2. God told employers not to "take advantage of" their workers (see 24:14). One way of taking advantage was delaying in paying wages. Can you think of any other ways in which an employer might take advantage of a worker?

Gleaning (24:19-22)

Ruth 2:1-23 describes an example of gleaning about three hundred years after Moses' death. According to Ruth 2:7-9, a landowner could decide who among the poor he would allow in his fields.

3. Describe the practice of leaving the "gleanings" of a harvest (see 24:19-22). How did it work?

4. How is the gleaning law an example of loving your neighbor?

5. The fourth commandment told Israel, "Six days you shall labor and do all your work" (5:13). How did the law of gleaning relate to the command to work?

6. How did the gleaning law uphold the right of property, the command not to steal (see 5:19)?

7. How do you think the gleaning laws affected the attitudes of . . .

   poor people (toward themselves, God, property owners, work)?

   property owners (toward themselves, God, the poor)?

8. Summarize what you think were the purposes of the gleaning law.

9. Does this law teach us anything that we could apply to the way we view and deal with poverty? If so, what does it teach?

Hospitality (23:24-25)

10. Consider the view of property behind 23:24-25.

a. What was a property owner's duty to travelers?

b. What was their duty to him?

In the dangerous world of Moses' day, when there were no inns or restaurants, this kind of hospitality was the only way any but rich travelers could survive. This law took "You shall not murder" (5:17) to the extreme of loving the neighbor by sustaining his life at one's own cost. It also protected the generous host from theft (see 5:19) or exploitation.

11. Do you think 23:24-25 suggests any ways Christians might love their neighbors (see Luke 10:25-37) and "practice hospitality" (Romans 12:13)? If so, how might it be adapted for modern situations? (Try to describe at least one principle or application or explain why you think the law is no longer relevant.)

The year of release (15:1-18)

Just as Israel was supposed to rest from work every seven days, so the people and the land were to rest every seven years (see Leviticus 25:1-7). In that year, no one was to plant any seed or harvest any crops. Landowners, landless poor, and even wild animals were allowed to live off whatever sprouted of itself or what they had saved over six years. Israel may have known that letting a field rest for a year let it regain fertility; Leviticus says only that the land belonged to the Lord.

Since people paid debts from the produce of their land or labor, they could not pay during a sabbath year. (Foreigners were not obliged to let their fields rest, so they were able to pay their debts, as Deuteronomy 15:3 requires.) Scholars debate

For Further Study: Jesus benefited from Deuteronomy 23:24-25 (see Luke 6:1-5), although He angered the Pharisees by doing so on the Sabbath. From what you know of Deuteronomy, why was Jesus' act perfectly appropriate on the Sabbath?

For Thought and Discussion: a. Why do you suppose the Lord reminded the Israelites so often in these passages that He had freed them from slavery (see 15:15; 24:18,22)?

b. What reminder should motivate Christians to love generously (see 1 John 3:16-18)?

whether Deuteronomy commands lenders to cancel debts or just to forego collection until the following year.[2]

The loans being canceled or postponed were emergency loans to the poor, not loans for business or large consumer goods. (See page 189. The whole study on loans in Optional Lesson D is relevant.)

12. The Scripture commands rest on the Sabbath in order to celebrate (1) God's rest after creating the world (see Exodus 20:11), and (2) the rest He gave His covenant people when He redeemed them from slavery (see Deuteronomy 5:15).

    a. How does canceling or postponing loans (see 15:1-3) celebrate man's participation in God's rest?

    b. How does the Sabbath year celebrate Israel's deliverance from slavery (see 15:1-3,12-15)?

Is sold to you (15:12). A poor person could oblige himself to work for six years to pay off a debt. This system differed from what we usually call slavery. See "Slavery in Israel" on page 200.

---

13. You might expect a person to be unwilling to lend in the fifth or sixth year, knowing that he might need that money in the year without income. God commanded both a behavior and an attitude in this case. Name each (see 15:7-11).

    behavior
    attitude

14. Why was it "sin" (15:9) to refuse to lend to a poor person? (Consider Deuteronomy 5:15,17,19,21; Luke 6:30-36.)

15. What did the Lord promise to the generous person (see 15:10)?

16. What attitudes (toward work, property, responsibility, oneself, one's master or servant) does 15:1-18 teach? Write down two or three.

17. Does 15:1-18 teach any attitudes that Christians should adopt and practice? If so, explain one of those attitudes and one way you can practice it.

18. Observe how the commandment not to steal is applied in each of the following passages. Then write down one way a modern person might apply the commandment in a similar way.

    19:14
    25:13-16

19. Summarize the attitude toward property you think the Lord is teaching in the passages in this lesson.

20. Read back over your answers in this lesson. Is there one particular attitude you believe you need to adopt or put into practice? If so, write down the truth you need to ponder, along with any concrete actions you might need to take in light of this truth.
    If you can think of no concrete action you want to take, write down the most important thing you learned from this lesson and at least one implication for your life.

21. List any questions you have about this study.

For the group

Warm-up. Let each person briefly explain how he or she tends to feel about property. To what extent do you feel that what's yours is yours? Who do you feel has the right to tell you what to do with your property? Don't worry at this point about what the New or Old Testament says; just let members voice the points of view they are starting with. Try not to approve or disapprove of anyone's opinion, and try to keep everyone to a one-minute speech.

Interpretation/Application. To keep political debate from sidetracking your discussion, define first what each law (on workers, gleaning, hospitality, loans, slavery) was. Then discuss the principles behind the laws, and the attitudes God might have been trying

For Thought and Discussion: a. What do you think were the *attitudes behind* and the *results of* Deuteronomy's provisions for the poor?

b. How were they like and unlike the attitudes and results of your country's welfare system?

c. What lessons for living the Ten Commandments might these laws in Deuteronomy offer modern lawmakers?

Optional Application: Choose one verse or paragraph from this lesson to meditate on for the next week. Which application of God's commands do you need to take to heart? Some possibilities are 15:10, 24:15, 25:13, and 25:16.

to teach. Use the Ten Commandments as a measuring standard. Then turn to how those principles and attitudes might be put into practice today.

Prayer.

Slavery in Israel

A slave is a person who is deprived of his freedom for a time, who is bought and sold, who is his master's property; "in this sense there were slaves in Israel, and some were Israelites."[3] But slavery in Israel was very different from slavery in early America or classical Rome.

The chief source of slaves in the ancient Near East was an international traffic in prisoners of war. The Lord permitted Israelites to enslave captured enemies from outside the Promised Land (see Deuteronomy 20:10-18) and to buy foreigners and aliens from slave traders (see Leviticus 25:44-45). A foreign slave was permanent property until sold. A male slave might be sold without his wife and children, and children of slaves automatically belonged to the master (see Exodus 21:4). However, God's Law protected even foreign slaves against extremes of cruelty (see Exodus 21:20-27). Although the Law recognized slaves as property, it also considered them human, unlike other Near Eastern codes.

The only lawful way for an Israelite to become a slave was if he or his relative fell into poverty (see Deuteronomy 15:1-3; 2 Kings 4:1-7; Isaiah 50:1). He was usually a defaulting debtor or the surety of a relative's bad debt. His creditor would buy him in exchange for the debt. However, he was bound for only six years, after which time his master had to free him (see Deuteronomy 15:12-15). While a slave, the Israelite had to be treated like a hired laborer (see Leviticus 25:39-41). The Israelite economy was not based on gangs of slaves as plantation economies have been; rather, slaves were treated as members of the family. They could be adopted and inherit property (see Proverbs 17:2). They shared in family worship and Sabbath rest (see Exodus 20:10; 23:12; Deuteronomy 12:12,18; 16:11,14). Their daily needs were guaranteed. Proverbs recommended harsh discipline for slaves as well as for sons (see Proverbs 13:24; 29:19,21), but God's Law set limits to cruelty.

1. Roland de Vaux, *Ancient Israel*, vol. 1 (New York: McGraw-Hill, 1965), 76.
2. J. A. Thompson, *Deuteronomy: An Introduction and Commentary* (London: InterVarsity, 1974), 185–188; Craigie, 236–238.
3. de Vaux, 80.

DEUTERONOMY 16:18-20; 17:2-20; 19:1-21; 21:1-9, 22-23; 24:16; 25:1-3

Justice in the Courts

"Follow justice and justice alone, so that you may live and possess the land the LORD your God is giving you."
                    Deuteronomy 16:20

Few of the people who debate modern legal systems know how many of their notions of justice come from the Old Testament. But there is even more to these laws. God's definitions of justice, atonement, guilt, and so on often reappear in the New Testament. Christ's work was in part a legal act based on these principles. Because the New and Old Testaments largely agree on what justice is, some of the questions in this lesson use New Testament cross-references.

As with all the optional lessons, feel free to omit some questions from this lessons.

For Thought and Discussion: Why do you think justice and prosperity were connected (see 16:20)?

For Thought and Discussion: Judges and rulers serve in God's name, by His authority (see Romans 13:1-2). How can a judge misuse God's name (see Deuteronomy 5:11)?

Judges (16:18-20)

1. What behavior did God demand of judges (see 16:18-20)?

2. What does *justice* mean in Scripture? Write down what the following verses reveal.

    Isaiah 28:17
    Romans 13:7
    Deuteronomy 5:6-21
    Deuteronomy 16:19

203

For Thought and Discussion: Our modern legal system follows 17:4,6. Do you think this is good? Why or why not?

For Thought and Discussion: Does 17:7 seem just to you? Why or why not?

For Thought and Discussion: Is 17:12-13 a principle we should apply in our legal system? Why or why not?

3. How can these passages guide Christians in electing, praying for, or being judges in our society? (Describe at least one specific way we can apply these verses.)

Verification (17:2-7)

God prescribed the death penalty for anyone convicted of pagan worship (see 13:1-18).

4. What principle of justice does 17:4 establish?

5. Why is it wise and just to require more than one witness to convict a person of a crime (see 17:6; 19:17)?

The hands of the witnesses (17:7). The witnesses threw the first stones so that if the accusation later proved false, the witnesses could be charged with murder.[1]

Referral (17:8-13)

If cases . . . are too difficult (17:8). In Israel, the priests at the central sanctuary were the supreme court, the final interpreters of Israel's constitution—the covenant law.

6. Why do you think the penalty for scorning final decisions was death (see 17:12-13)? (Consider what this contempt said about God.)

Kings (17:14-20)

God knew even at this time that Israel would demand a king like the other nations (see 1 Samuel 8:19-20). Although He wanted His people to rely on Him as their King, He gave laws that would make plain the sins of future kinds. Liberal scholars feel that 17:14-20 so exactly describes what Israel's kings actually did, that it must have been written after those kings reigned.

7. What desires most tempted oriental kings (see 17:16-17)?

8. The king was supposed to read God's Word every day to avoid two common wrong attitudes. What were they?

   17:19
   17:20

9. Do attitudes and desires like these tempt modern leaders? If so, what can leaders and people do about these temptations?

Testimony (19:15-21)

False testimony broke not only the ninth commandment (see 5:20) but also the third (see 5:11), since the oath was taken in God's name.

10. How did God try to prevent people from giving false testimony (see 19:15-21)?

11. Why is false testimony so serious?

12. How can a Christian avoid accusing someone falsely?

For Thought and Discussion: How are Christians tempted to bear false testimony at work, among friends, at church?

Optional Application: Have you accused someone falsely? If so, confess to God and ask Him whether and how you can make restitution.

Optional Application: Ask God to deliver your church from the temptation to accuse falsely. Make this a persistent prayer.

For Thought and Discussion: To what extent is the principle of the punishment fitting the crime (see 19:21) a just standard for our legal system? How should it be applied to specific crimes?

Life for life, eye for eye (19:21). This law was meant to achieve justice for everyone. False witnesses were to have penalties in proportion to the seriousness of their lies. They were not to be vengefully killed for exposing someone to a fine, nor just be fined when they accused someone of murder.

Fines were much more common in Israel than literal maiming; "eye for eye" was a figure of speech. In fact, the only case of actual body mutilation in the Law is Deuteronomy 25:11-12, whereas it was extremely common elsewhere in the Near East. God's principle of justice was *proportionate restitution*, not vengeance.[2]

**Optional
Application:** Does
Matthew 5:38-42
suggest anything
you should do? If so,
what?

For Further Study:
When someone
harmed another in
the ancient Near
East, the offended
one frequently took
revenge on the
whole family of the
offender.[4] How did
God change the
accepted notions of
justice in 24:16?

**For Thought and
Discussion:** How
could we apply the
principles of 25:1-3
to our own system of
penalties?

**For Thought and
Discussion:** Are the
laws of murder and
refuge relevant to our
legal system in any
ways? If so, how? If
not, why not?

13. Read Matthew 5:38-42. Do you think Jesus
means that the penalty for false witnesses (see
Deuteronomy 19:21) is unjust or unloving? If
so, how do you think He would advise societies
to deal with false witnesses? If not, explain
what application of the eye-for-eye rule He does
denounce.

Punishment (24:16; 25:1-3)

Beaten (25:2). In Moses' day, imprisonment was
impractical and rare; beating with a rod was
standard. Many societies permitted authori-
ties to beat slaves, wives, children, and criminals as much as they saw fit. The Babylonian
Code of Hammurabi permitted sixty lashes for
criminals.[3]

14. What principles of justice and attitudes toward
human beings do you see in 25:1-3?

Murder (19:1-21; 21:1-9)

Three cities (19:2). The cities of refuge that were
mentioned in 4:41-43. These cities were meant
to protect a person who killed someone by acci-
dent, so that the dead man's kinsmen would not
take revenge before the trial (see 19:4-6).

15. How do the laws regarding murder and refuge
(see 19:1-13) uphold the value of human life?

    the life of the victim
    the life of the accused

Atonement (21:8). Literally, "covering over" or
"blotting out" by making satisfaction for a
wrong done.[5]

Read what Israel was supposed to do when a person was found killed by an unknown murderer (see 21:1-9). According to the principle of life for life, a murderer had to die for his crime. Without restitution, there was no justice. The "avenger of blood" (19:6,12), the dead man's next of kin, would hold the nearest town responsible. He might demand a human life from that town in satisfaction.

16. How did God provide that (a) the just consequence of murder would be fulfilled, but (b) no person from the town would have to bear the town's responsibility (see 21:1-9)?

17. How was Jesus' death like the rite in Deuteronomy 21:1-9? (Compare Deuteronomy 21:8-9 to Romans 3:23-26.)

Hung on a tree (21:22). The bodies of executed criminals were often hung on poles, trees, or walls as public warnings.

---

18. What attitude towards criminals lies behind 21:22-23?

19. In Romans 6:23, Paul says that all who sin deserve death. In Galatians 3:10, he says that those who acknowledge God's Law but do not obey it are under God's curse.
    According to Deuteronomy 21:23 and Galatians 3:13, why was Jesus hung up on a cross in public view?

20. What is the most significant truth about God, justice, or Jesus' work that you saw in this study?

21. Does anything you learned in this study have implications for your life? Write down any implications you can think of.

22. List any questions you have about this lesson.

For Further Study: Many of the laws in this lesson served to train God's people to abandon private vengeance in favor of justice and public legal procedures. You can study in the New Testament how Jesus built on this standard of *justice* to teach us to go beyond it to *love*. See Matthew 5:44; 18:15-20; Luke 17:3-4; Romans 12:17-21; 1 Corinthians 6:7.

For the group

Warm-up. Let members share in a couple of sentences one thing they think is good and one they think is bad about your country's legal system.

Summarize the overall point of this lesson. You'll notice two strands: principles of justice that we could apply today, and principles that explain what Jesus did for us.

Justice. From the passages in this lesson, you can make three lists: principles of justice, the Lord's values and priorities, and the Lord's character traits.

When you discuss applications, try not to be sidetracked into an argument over capital punishment unless you have researched the New Testament perspective on this subject. Genesis 9:4-7 also discusses the value God places on human life.

Be sure to allow time to examine how Jesus' death reflects Deuteronomy 21:1-9,22-23.

Prayer.

1. J. A. Thompson, *Deuteronomy: An Introduction and Commentary* (London: InterVarsity, 1974), 201.
2. Thompson, 218; Craigie, 270; Roland de Vaux, *Ancient Israel*, vol. 1 (New York: McGraw-Hill, 1965), 149, 159–160.
3. Peter C. Craigie, *The Book of Deuteronomy* (Grand Rapids, MI: Eerdmans, 1976), 312.
4. Thompson, 247–248; de Vaux, 11.
5. William Owen Carver, "Atonement," *The International Standard Bible Encyclopedia*, vol. 1, 321–324.

DEUTERONOMY 20:1-20; 21:10-23; 22:1-30; 23:1-8; 24:1-5,7; 25:5-12,17-19

War, Women, Kindness, Crime

"Follow justice and justice alone."
Deuteronomy 16:20

The laws in this lesson cover an assortment of topics because they fall outside the main categories of religious, economic, and judicial law. However, they still show us principles of God's justice and compassion that suggest examples for us to follow.

The holy war (20:1-20)

Murder—unlawful killing—was forbidden, since only the Giver of Life had authority to say when to take it. However, as in the cases of idolatry and murder, the "just war" was not only lawful but even commanded killing. (Recall that not every war Israel might have liked to fight was lawful [see 1:41–2:9]; the holy war was unique.)

1. Because only wars that God had specifically commanded were supposed to be fought, what attitude should the warriors have (see 20:1-4)?

For Thought and Discussion: Why do you suppose an army fighting for the Lord could afford to exempt so many men (see 20:5-8)?

For Further Study: Notice how soldiers were told to treat trees while laying siege (see 20:19-20). What values do you think lay behind this command? Does it seem strange to you that God made rules to protect trees? Why or why not?

For Thought and Discussion: Why do you think God didn't simply forbid taking captives and give men and women equal legal status?

Study Skill—Application

If you choose a verse such as 20:4 to memorize, take care to remember its context and to apply it only to modern situations that are truly comparable. In the case of the holy war, for instance, God will fight *if* He has commanded the battle. Also, read Old Testament passages like this one in light of New Testament passages such as Matthew 5:43-48, 2 Corinthians 10:3-5, and Ephesians 6:10-13.

2. Observe who was exempt from military service (see 20:5-8). What views of life's priorities did these exemptions show? (That is, what was more important than war?)

Women (21:10-1; 22:13-19; 24:1-5)

As your wife (21:11). In most ancient societies, women were lower than cattle. Conquered women were taken for sex, then put to work as slaves.

3. What did God say about enslaving a woman after sleeping with her (see 21:14)?

Shave her head . . . wearing when captured (21:12-13). These actions probably served both as mourning rites and as signs that she was renouncing her pagan life and accepting the Lord's covenant life. Compare Ephesians 4:22-24.

4. Why do you think God required a man to let a captive woman mourn for a month before consummating a marriage (see 21:13)?

5. What attitudes toward women would 21:10-14 have encouraged in Israelite men?

Proof of her virginity (22:14). Two explanations for this phrase have been offered. If a bride was bleeding monthly, then she was of age, fertile, and not pregnant.[1] Alternatively, blood from a broken hymen on the wedding night would have proven that she had never had relations before. However, the absence of blood would not have proven her guilt, since hymens break for many reasons.

---

6. What injustices did 22:13-21 protect against?

Certificate of divorce (24:1). According to Jesus (see Matthew 19:8), God permitted legal divorce to prevent men from abandoning their wives.

---

7. a. The Lord allowed divorce and remarriage in most cases, but in what case did He forbid it (see 24:1-4)?

   b. Why do you think He forbade it in this case?

8. What can the laws about women tell us about God?

Capital crimes (21:18-21; 22:20-30)

Like the other capital crimes, these crimes hark back to the Ten Commandments (see 5:16-18). In practice, circumstances often moved Israel's judges to reduce death sentences to lesser penalties. The reduced sentence was mercy, not strict justice; the deserved penalty reflected the severity with which God viewed these sins.

9. a. Describe the criminal for whom 21:18-21 commands death.

   b. Why did this crime deserve stoning? (Consider the effect this person would have on society, and his overall attitude toward God and neighbor.)

For Further Study: Deuteronomy taught Israel not to take divorce lightly (see 22:19; 24:1-4). Study how Jesus took this lesson further in Matthew 19:1-12.

For Further Study: List all the crimes for which the penalty was death. Then match each with one or more of the Ten Commandments.

For Thought and Discussion: Why do you think the two parents' witness was sufficient to convict their son (see 21:18-21)?

211

10. Read carefully the crimes that demanded stoning in 22:13-27. Why did these felons deserve death under God's standard of justice (see 5:18)?

He must marry the girl (22:29). It might seem that the command of 22:28-29 punished the victim as much as the attacker. However, in the Near East, no man would have taken a wife who had been raped. She was considered worthless. This law required the rapist to pay her bride price and take responsibility for supporting her.

As Jesus said regarding divorce (see Matthew 19:8), God could not give perfectly just laws to sinful people.

---

11. Why do you think Deuteronomy 24:7 was a capital crime?

12. The Law declared that rebellion against parents, adultery, rape, kidnapping, idolatry (see 13:1-18), and showing contempt for legal decisions (see 17:12) were all crimes worthy of death, just as murder was.

How should this declaration affect our own view of these crimes?

Exclusion from Israel (23:1-8; 25:17-19)

The assembly of the LORD (23:1). His covenant people, full Israelites who could participate fully in His worship. Resident aliens, for instance, had rights but were not members of the covenant.[2] Adult Israelite women were members of the covenant but did not share in decision-making on a par with the men.

This word *assembly* was translated *ekklesia* in the Greek Old Testament. In the apostle Paul's writings, *ekklesia* is rendered *church* in most English versions.

Some people think the "assembly" was only the governing elders of Israel, not the congregation of all full citizens.

13. Two kinds of Israelites were excluded from the assembly: emasculated men and people of illegitimate birth (see 23:1-2). What might God have been trying to teach about Himself and the covenant assembly by these laws?

For Thought and Discussion: On what basis do the excluded overcome the Law's barriers to joining the assembly (see Isaiah 56:4,6; Acts 10:35)?

Tenth generation (23:3). Virtually forever. Compare "as long as you live" (literally, "all your days forever" in 23:6.[3]

Third generation (23:3). For some reason, Edom and Egypt were less abhorrent than Ammon and Moab.

---

14. Read the attitudes the Lord commanded concerning Amalek, Ammon, Moab, Edom, and Egypt (see 23:3-8, 25:17-19). What might God have been trying to teach by commanding Israel to discriminate among peoples for membership in the assembly?

15. Ruth, King David's great-grandmother, was from Moab. Matthew makes a point of this in his genealogy of Jesus (see Matthew 1:5). In light of Deuteronomy 23:3-6, why is it significant that Israel's kings and Messiah descended from a Moabitess?

16. What has happened to the laws of exclusion from the assembly (church) in the new covenant (see Isaiah 56:3-8; Acts 8:26-39)?

17. One purpose of the Old Testament laws of exclusion was to point to an important New Testament truth. What is that truth? (*Optional*: See Acts 10:34-35; Romans 3:27-31; Galatians 3:26-29; Ephesians 2:11-22.)

18. How should we respond as Christians to the way God has overturned the laws of Deuteronomy 23:1-8?

Kindness (22:1-4)

Deuteronomy 22:1-4 is case law—sample situations of loving one's neighbor to show how the ethical principle should work in practice.

19. Describe a recent time when you have faced a situation like the ones in 22:1-4. If you can't recall one, describe a similar situation that you might face.

The Torah today

20. What new insights about the Lord or Old Testament justice seem most significant to you currently?

21. Does anything in this study have implications for the issues and situations you confront in your life? Have you been challenged to change an attitude or a habit? If so, write down those implications and anything you plan to do about them.

22. List any questions you have about this lesson.

For the group

Because this lesson covers a variety of unconnected laws, you may find it difficult to give focus to your discussion. One tactic would be to go through each section—the holy war, capital crimes, women, exclusion from Israel, and kindness—and ask two questions: (1) Was there anything in the passage or the questions that members found difficult? and (2) What did members learn about the Lord or justice from the passage? Then give members a chance to say what seemed most significant to them in this lesson and what implications they see for their lives.

1. J. A. Thompson, *Deuteronomy: An Introduction and Commentary* (London: InterVarsity, 1974), 235–236.
2. Peter C. Craigie, *The Book of Deuteronomy* (Grand Rapids, MI: Eerdmans, 1976), 296; Thompson, 238.
3. Kenneth Barker, ed., *The NIV Study Bible* (Grand Rapids, MI: Zondervan, 1985), 272.

GOING ON IN DEUTERONOMY

If your study of Deuteronomy has sparked your interest in the Old Testament, here are some ideas for further study.

1. Read more details of Israel's escape from Egypt and the covenant at Sinai in the book of Exodus.

2. Read about the desert wandering in Numbers.

3. Study Moses' character as he matured from Egyptian prince to desert leader in Exodus and Numbers.

4. Compare the laws in Exodus 20:22–23:19 to Deuteronomy 12:1–26:19.

5. Find the following places in the New Testament where Jesus, Paul, or someone else quotes Deuteronomy. What light do the New and Old Testament contexts of the same verses shed on each other?

Matthew 4:4,7,10	Romans 13:9
Matthew 5:17-20	Romans 15:10
Matthew 5:21,27,31,33,38	1 Corinthians 5:13
Matthew 15:4	1 Corinthians 9:9
Matthew 19:18-19	2 Corinthians 13:1
Matthew 22:24	Galatians 3:10-13
Matthew 22:37	Ephesians 6:2-3
Acts 3:22-23	1 Timothy 5:18
Acts 7:37	Hebrews 1:6
Romans 7:7	Hebrews 10:30
Romans 10:5-8	Hebrews 12:21,29
Romans 10:19	Hebrews 13:5
Romans 11:8	James 2:11
Romans 12:19	

STUDY AIDS

For further information on the material in this study, consider the following sources. They are available on the Internet (www.christianbook.com, www .amazon.com, and so on), or your local Christian bookstore should be able to order any of them if it does not carry them. Most seminary libraries have them, as well as many university and public libraries. If they are out of print, you might be able to find them online.

Commentaries on Deuteronomy

Currid, John D. *Deuteronomy: EP Study Commentary*. (Evangelical Press, 2006).
    In this serious commentary from a Reformed perspective, Currid uses his own translation from the original Hebrew to demonstrate that the book of Deuteronomy is an official document ratifying the formal covenant relationship between God as the sovereign King and His covenant people, Israel. At more than 600 pages, this volume is thorough and might not be the best choice for new Bible students, but people who want a comprehensive verse-by-verse treatment may find this resource to be exactly what they need.

Longman III, Tremper. *Deuteronomy Thru Ruth: The Importance of Obedience*. (Barbour Publishing, 2009).
    Part of the QUICKNOTES SIMPLIFIED BIBLE COMMENTARY series, this is an accessible reference designed for everyday Christians. It is especially helpful for personal Bible study or Sunday school preparation. Along with the themes, historical and literary contexts, major interpretations on controversial passages, and explanations of puzzling passages and Bible practices that you'd expect to find in any commentary, this handy volume also offers practical applications for each passage.

Walton, John H., David W. Baker, and Daniel I. Block. *Zondervan Illustrated Bible Backgrounds Commentary*, Vol. 1 Genesis, Exodus, Leviticus, Numbers, and Deuteronomy. (Zondervan, 2009).
    This scholarly and comprehensive introduction to the first five books of the Bible also happens to be beautifully illustrated. Covers major issues

such as translation, chronology and authorship in detail via a passage-by-passage commentary.

Wiersbe, Warren W. *Be Equipped* (Deuteronomy). (David C. Cook, 2010).
Respected pastor and Bible teacher Warren Wiersbe offers this updated volume in the popular BE commentary series. Filled with practical insights and fresh perspectives, this study focuses on the importance of a believer's obedience and its connection to experiencing God's best in our lives.

Miscellaneous resources

Towns, Elmer L. *Praying for Your Second Chance* (Destiny Image, 2009).
Definitely not a commentary or other typical Bible study resource, this unique book by respected Liberty University professor and prayer leader Elmer Towns leads you in praying the truths of Deuteronomy into your life. If you want to have a heart experience to support the intellectual stimulation of Deuteronomy, this is a great book to add to your library—and to use.

Histories, concordances, dictionaries, and encyclopedias

A **history** or **survey** traces Israel's history from beginning to end so that you can see where each biblical event fits. *A Survey of Israel's History* by Leon Wood (Zondervan, 1970) is a good basic introduction for laymen from a conservative viewpoint. Not critical or heavily learned, but not simplistic. Many other good histories are available.

A **concordance** lists words of the Bible alphabetically along with each verse in which the word appears. It lets you do your own word studies. An *exhaustive* concordance lists every word used in a given translation, while an *abridged* or *complete* concordance omits either some words, some occurrences of the word, or both.

Two of the best exhaustive concordances are *Strong's Exhaustive Concordance* and *The Strongest NIV Exhaustive Concordance*. *Strong's* is available based on the King James Version of the Bible and the New American Standard Bible. *Strong's* has an index by which you can find out which Greek or Hebrew word is used in a given English verse. The NIV concordance does the same thing except it also includes an index for Aramaic words in the original texts from which the NIV was translated. However, neither concordance requires knowledge of the original languages. *Strong's* is available online at www.biblestudytools.com. Both are also available in hard copy.

A **Bible dictionary** or **Bible encyclopedia** alphabetically lists articles about people, places, doctrines, important words, customs, and geography of the Bible.

Holman Illustrated Bible Dictionary, by C. Brand, C. W. Draper, and A. England (B&H, 2003), offers more than seven hundred color photos, illustrations, and charts; sixty full-color maps; and up-to-date archeological findings, along with exhaustive definitions of people, places, things, and events—dealing with every subject in the Bible. It uses a variety of Bible translations and is the only dictionary that includes the HCSB, NIV, KJV, RSV, NRSV, REB, NASB, ESV, and TEV.

The New Unger's Bible Dictionary, Revised and Expanded, by Merrill F. Unger (Moody, 2006), has been a best seller for almost fifty years. Its 6,700-plus entries reflect the most current scholarship and more than 1,200,000 words are supplemented with detailed essays, colorful photography and maps, and dozens of charts and illustrations to enhance your understanding of God's Word. Based on the New American Standard Version.

The Zondervan Encyclopedia of the Bible, edited by Moisés Silva and Merrill C. Tenney (Zondervan, 2008), is excellent and exhaustive. However, its five 1,000-page volumes are a financial investment, so all but very serious students may prefer to use it at a church, public, college, or seminary library.

Unlike a Bible dictionary in the above sense, *Vine's Complete Expository Dictionary of Old and New Testament Words,* by W. E. Vine, Merrill F. Unger, and William White Jr. (Thomas Nelson, 1996), alphabetically lists major words used in the King James Version and defines each Old Testament Hebrew or New Testament Greek word the KJV translates with that English word. *Vine's* lists verse references where that Hebrew or Greek word appears so that you can do your own cross-references and word studies without knowing the original languages.

The Brown-Driver-Briggs Hebrew and English Lexicon by Francis Brown, C. Briggs, and S. R. Driver (Hendrickson, 1996), is probably the most respected and comprehensive Bible lexicon for Old Testament studies. *BDB* gives not only dictionary definitions for each word but relates each word to its Old Testament usage and categorizes its nuances of meaning.

Bible atlases and map books

A **Bible atlas** can be a great aid to understanding what is going on in a book of the Bible and how geography affected events. Here are a few good choices:

The Hammond Atlas of Bible Lands (Langenscheidt, 2007) packs a ton of resources into just sixty-four pages. Maps, of course, but also photographs, illustrations, and a comprehensive timeline. Includes an introduction to the unique geography of the Holy Land, including terrain, trade routes, vegetation, and climate information.

The New Moody Atlas of the Bible, by Barry J. Beitzel (Moody, 2009), is scholarly, very evangelical, and full of theological text, indexes, and references. Beitzel shows vividly how God prepared the land of Israel perfectly for the acts of salvation He was going to accomplish in it.

Then and Now Bible Maps Insert (Rose, 2008) is a nifty paperback that is sized just right to fit inside your Bible cover. Only forty-four pages long, it features clear plastic overlays of modern-day cities and countries so you can see what nation or city now occupies the Bible setting you are reading about. Every major city of the Bible is included.

For small-group leaders

Discipleship Journal's Best Small-Group Ideas, Volumes 1 and 2 (NavPress, 2005).
Each volume is packed with 101 of the best hands-on tips and group-building principles from *Discipleship Journal's* "Small Group Letter" and "DJ Plus" as well as articles from the magazine. They will help you inject new passion into the life of your small group.

Donahue, Bill. *Leading Life-Changing Small Groups* (Zondervan, 2002).
This comprehensive resource is packed with information, practical tips, and insights that will teach you about small-group philosophy and structure, discipleship, conducting meetings, and more.

McBride, Neal F. *How to Build a Small-Groups Ministry* (NavPress, 1994).
How to Build a Small-Groups Ministry is a time-proven, hands-on workbook for pastors and lay leaders that includes everything you need to know to develop a plan that fits your unique church. Through basic principles, case studies, and worksheets, McBride leads you through twelve logical steps for organizing and administering a small-groups ministry.

McBride, Neal F. *How to Lead Small Groups* (NavPress, 1990).
This book covers leadership skills for all kinds of small groups: Bible study, fellowship, task, and support groups. Filled with step-by-step guidance and practical exercises to help you grasp the critical aspects of small-group leadership and dynamics.

Miller, Tara, and Jenn Peppers. *Finding the Flow: A Guide for Leading Small Groups and Gatherings* (IVP Connect, 2008).
Finding the Flow offers a fresh take on leading small groups by seeking to develop the leader's small-group facilitation skills.

Bible study methods

Discipleship Journal's Best Bible Study Methods (NavPress, 2002).
This is a collection of thirty-two creative ways to explore Scripture that will help you enjoy studying God's Word more.

Hendricks, Howard, and William Hendricks. *Living by the Book: The Art and Science of Reading the Bible* (Moody, 2007).
Living by the Book offers a practical three-step process that will help you master simple yet effective inductive methods of observation,

interpretation, and application that will make all the difference in your time with God's Word. A workbook by the same title is also available to go along with the book.

The Navigator Bible Studies Handbook (NavPress, 1994).
This resource teaches the underlying principles for doing good inductive Bible study, including instructions on doing question-and-answer studies, verse-analysis studies, chapter-analysis studies, and topical studies.

Warren, Rick. *Rick Warren's Bible Study Methods: Twelve Ways You Can Unlock God's Word* (HarperCollins, 2006)
Rick Warren offers simple, step-by-step instructions, guiding you through twelve different approaches to studying the Bible for yourself with the goal of becoming more like Jesus.